P 27.
P 55-56.
P 63.
P 88
P 95.
P 105.

LAUGH WITH
THE COMEDIANS

60p

LAUGH WITH

THE COMEDIANS

By KEN IRWIN

Published by WOLFE PUBLISHING LIMITED
10 EARLHAM STREET, LONDON WC2
in association with INDEPENDENT TELEVISION
BOOKS LIMITED, publishers of TV TIMES

ISBN 72340489 5

Made and Printed in Great Britain
by C. Nicholls and Company Ltd.

CONTENTS

	Page
Chapter One **How it all Started**	7
Chapter Two **Steve Faye**	19
Chapter Three **Ken Goodwin**	29
Chapter Four **Frank Carson**	35
Chapter Five **Colin Crompton**	43
Chapter Six **Charlie Williams**	51
Chapter Seven **Tom O'Connor**	59
Chapter Eight **Jos White**	67
Chapter Nine **Bernard Manning**	73
Chapter Ten **George Roper**	83
Chapter Eleven **Mike Burton**	91
Chapter Twelve **Mike Reid**	99
Chapter Thirteen **Bryn Phillips**	111
Chapter Fourteen **Syd Francis**	119

Photographs, unless otherwise acknowledged, by courtesy of Granada Television

CONTENTS (continued)

Page

Chapter Fifteen
Dave Butler   125

Chapter Sixteen
Sammy Thomas   131

Chapter Seventeen
Alan Fox   135

Chapter Eighteen
Tony Stewart   141

Chapter Nineteen
Duggie Brown   147

Chapter Twenty
A Last Laugh   155
with
Jackie Hamilton
Bal Moane
Johnny (Goon) Tweed
Mike Coyne
Eddie Flanagan
Hector Nicol
Pat Mooney
Stu Francis
Paddy Cassidy
Paul Melba
Johnny Wager
Johnny More
Bobby Knoxall
Colin Price

Chapter One
HOW IT ALL STARTED

I HAD NEVER seen a chair collapse through laughter before . . . until that day when Alec Todd suddenly fell on the floor with a dull thud, and we all laughed hysterically.

It happened in the most unlikely place, too. In the austere, high-ceilinged halls of the Montreux Casino in Switzerland. There was only a handful of us there. Some directors and programme controllers from various ITV companies, and their wives, half-a-dozen Pressmen and TV critics.

The occasion was a sneak preview of a new pilot TV programme, tentatively called *The Comedians*.

John Hamp, the producer of the show, was there, anxiously waiting for the verdict of this first and ultra-critical audience. So was Denis Forman, Granada's managing director, who clearly was knocked out of his stride when Mr. Todd collapsed in a heap on the floor only ten minutes after the programme had started.

I was sitting immediately behind Mr. Todd, who is a big man of 15 stone or more, and an executive with Granada's closest ITV rival, Yorkshire TV.

The laughs for *The Comedians* were slow to come at first, because no one was quite sure whether this new format – which was simply a parade of Northern club comedians – would work.

New comedians, too, most of them. Unknown faces. Strangers to TV. But then, as the jokes came thick and fast, I saw from the rear Alec's huge shoulders heave and retract several times. And then it happened. There was a slow, splintering sound. The huge man began to tilt sideways. One leg of the chair went completely, and Todd dropped, like a felled tree, onto the floor with a resounding crash.

The disintegrating chair was the highspot of the afternoon. It was the man-slipping-on-a-banana-skin joke, only for real! I felt sorry for Denis Forman, having to follow Alec's tumble with a brief 'speech' about the new programme. It wasn't easy.

Alec himself was not very amused. When the laughter had died down, and I asked him later how he felt, he said with a wry chuckle: 'It's all very well, you lot laughing . . . but I could have broken my bloody neck!'

Someone in the Palace Hotel bar that night, said jokingly: 'I don't know! The lengths Yorkshire TV will go to in order to upstage Granada!'

The truth of course was that Alec Todd couldn't stop himself laughing that afternoon. Like the rest of us, he had been made to laugh like he'd never laughed for a very long time. There are not many laughs in Montreux, believe me. It's that sort of place.

And when I later asked Philip Jones, light entertainment chief for Thames TV, what he thought of Granada's new comedy product, he said, I thought with a tinge of envy, 'Well, it's extremely funny, isn't it? It's terrific!'

It was the simplest format ever devised for a TV comedy show. Johnnie Hamp rounded up a group of ten comedians, most of them familiar on the boozy Northern nightclub circuit, put them in front of the TV camera in a 15-minute spot each, and let them tell their best favourite jokes.

Then, with director Wally Butler, the show was edited down, cutting out all the build-up to the jokes, all the flannel, and leaving in just the gags themselves – with some of the studio applause!

Hamp, a Cockney by birth, has always had a soft spot for a comic, ever since his own days on the halls. His father, Bill, was on the stage as a magician under the name of The Great Hamp, and Johnnie, as a schoolboy, used to help him with the act.

When he was 17, Johnnie went out on his own with a song-and-dance act. After service in the RAF he quit the stage to go into theatre management and joined the Granada cinema chain. He started at the Granada, Kingston, moved on to work in the head office, and then went on tour, producing one-night rock 'n' roll stage shows with Terry Dene, Cliff Richard and the rest of the guitar-strumming Rockers.

Moving into television, he joined Granada in Manchester and became a producer. Johnnie was the first producer to really give

8

Steve Faye and Mike Burton are introduced to the Queen by Bernard Delfont at the Liverpool Royal Show

The Beatles their big TV break, in the early 1960's. He later produced TV musical specials with Lennon and McCartney, Ella Fitzgerald, Burt Bacharach and Count Basie.

As Head of Light Entertainment for Granada, Johnnie was asked, early in 1971, to find a new comedy series for TV. This was easier said than done, of course. He had been interested in comedians ever since being on stage himself. 'I'd stood for hours in the wings, watching comics working, and being totally fascinated with their varying styles,' Johnnie told me.

But the thing that really gave him an insight into comedy, and taught him that people must often learn to laugh at adversity, came when his own 'teenage daughter Merry was blinded in a school laboratory accident. For years, doctors have tried to revive her sight with a series of eye operations.

In 1968, Johnnie spent nearly the whole year away from his job, trying to comfort his sightless daughter in a Spanish hospital. 'To keep her going, I had to read to her every day,' he recalls. 'I read more than 250 books to her, to help keep up her spirits. They were mostly comedy books, to help her to laugh. More books than I'd ever read in my whole life before.'

'This period, above everything else, taught me that you've got to laugh at life, no matter what may happen. And you've sometimes got to laugh at your own problems.'

This is significant because with the fantastic success of *The Comedians* as a TV show, Hamp could easily now be accused, in some quarters, of encouraging comedians to tell jokes which might possibly upset some people in certain situations or circumstances. Jokes, for instance, about personal physical defects. People who stutter, people who limp, deaf people. This hit him hardest, he confesses, when he started to hear jokes coming in about people being shortsighted.

'There is a very narrow dividing line between a joke which is in bad taste and a joke which is acceptable,' insists Hamp. 'Just as there is a border-line between a dirty joke and a clean one. It all depends on how it's told. Two comics can tell the same joke, and one will be lewd and objectionable, and the other one clean and funny.'

Johnnie was fortunate, too, in finding Wally Butler, a Granada director who was steeped in the tradition of music hall. His father was a comedian, Wal Butler, and his mother was Ida Lyndon, a soubrette, and Wally was born in Glasgow while his father was playing Buttons in the pantomime *Cinderella*. It was only natural that he should follow in the family theatri-

Anita Harris and Danny La Rue present Ken Goodwin with the Bernard Delfont Supreme Award at *The Stage and Television Today* presentation

cal tradition, and he became an entertainer too. He formed a double act with John Beattie, calling themselves Beattie and Butler. Wally played the piano, and Beattie did most of the comedy.

After the act broke up, Wally moved into Scottish TV, wrote scripts for *The One O'Clock Gang Show* for four years, and acted as 'feed' to various comics in Scotland.

He has been with Granada TV for eight years, directed *Coronation Street* for nearly three, and is now thoroughly at home dealing with dyed-in-the-wool comedians.

Once the comedians turn up at the studios for recordings, it's the job of Lucinda Bradbury, John Hamp's secretary for nearly five years, to look after them, keep them happy, make sure they remain in a jovial frame of mind before each taping.

This is an important behind-the-scenes function, because most comedians are notorious worriers. 'Fortunately,' says Lucinda, 'these fellows have been around quite a bit, and after mixing with tough nightclub audiences, they seem to find the atmosphere of a TV studio much more relaxing.'

Most of the comedians playing the clubs, Hamp had known a long time. But were they suitable for television? That was his first big worry. For years, TV producers had been turning down club comedians, mainly because most of them were rather 'blue' or downright dirty in their material. Only a handful ever escaped from the clubs and really made it on TV . . . Comics like Jimmy Tarbuck, Johnny Hackett, Ray Fell, Les Dawson and Freddie Davies.

The main problem facing Hamp and Butler was that they knew these fellows could be funny in the clubs – but could they be funny on TV, away from the pint pots, the beer, crisps and hot meat pies? Did they have enough 'clean' material which would be acceptable to a TV family audience?

'We also didn't know whether they could work together,' admitted Johnnie. 'Getting ten comics together at the same time in the studio and putting them in one show worried me. I didn't know if they'd all hit it off.' As things turned out, they did.

There were, of course, the exceptions. Those who have since made it big on TV are now laughing all the way to the bank. Others, who tried, but didn't make it, went back to the clubs. For there has been a mad scramble by comedians all over Britain to get on the the TV bandwagon since *The Comedians* was launched, in June 1971.

12

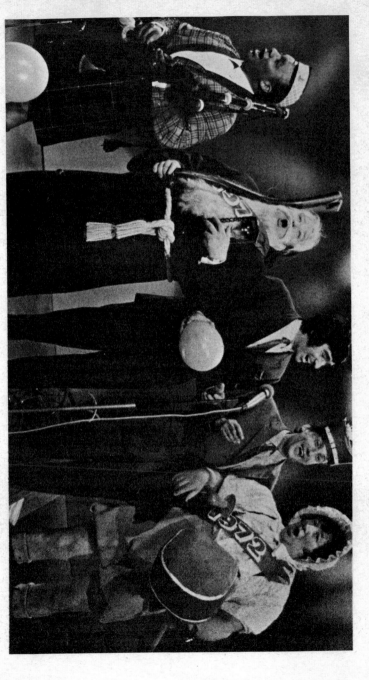

Happy New Year – The Comedians welcome 1972 with Jos White in his kilt, Bernard Manning as Old Father Time, Ken Goodwin, Colin Crompton and the New Year Babe, George Roper

Granada TV – and other TV companies, as well – have been inundated with letters and phone calls from would-be funnymen all bent on proving they're as comical as any of the blokes on the TV show.

Hamp originally set out to find thirty comedians with enough useable material to sustain a TV series for at least six weeks. The fact that it is still running – and promises to be for some years yet – pleases and also surprises him.

He would have been happy with one full, successful series out of the comedians. Instead, the show has proved a winner in every sense of the word. An absolute barnstormer.

The TV critics raved about it almost without exception. From the Communist *Morning Star* to *The Times* for Top People, they all fell about laughing. And Hamp's merry band of laughter-makers have shot from obscurity to stardom, all within the space of twelve months.

Peter Black, Trojan critic of the *Daily Mail*, wrote: 'The Comedians is the newest attempt to bring stand-up joke comedy to television, and by far the most successful . . . Sharp cutting kept the pace. At its best the show created a huge golden ball of laughter which the comedians seemed to shove higher with each gag. I felt energised with laughter.'

Henry Raynor, writing in *The Times*, said: 'It has all the charm of the old world in which comedians were expected to make you laugh simply by being funny men.'

Matthew Coady of the *Daily Mirror* wrote: 'If you have a weakness for stories about false teeth, parrots and plumbers, and men who die through drinking bottles of varnish (they have a lovely finish!) then this is for you. For my part, I wouldn't have missed it.'

The *Morning Star* said: 'Very, very, very funny. Please watch it!' And James Towler in *The Stage and Television Today* wrote: 'Where they have triumphed is in the sheer simplicity of their approach. No gimmicks. No fancy sets. None of the patronising attitude found in the big star spectaculars. Just a handful of extremely capable club comedians doing their own thing, backed by some very clever editing.'

The Comedians has created new frontiers in the world of TV, and has fiercely smashed down a lot of barriers in the field of comedy. Johnny Speight, first with his Alf Garnett, then with Spike Milligan blacked up as an Irish Pakistani in *Curry and Chips*, laughed at race relations in situation-comedy settings. Now *The Comedians* has taken the whole thing one step further.

Shep's Banjo Boys – the lads who introduce the show with 'When You're Smiling'

They brought on real coloured men, not just blacked-up white men, and let them tell racial jokes. Blatant racial jokes, more often aimed at their own races. And audiences all over the country, black as well as pink and varying shades in between, have been laughing as well. Or so we're told.

It was labelled Black Comedy. But comedians like Charlie Williams, Sammy Thomas and Jos White now thrive on every shaded, off-colour laugh-line. They appear to honestly believe that they are doing more to help race relations than to hinder. And Hamp sticks by them in this philosophy.

When Bernard Manning went on TV in a documentary programme and said that the first Pakistani or Indian comedian would make a fortune, he meant it. Shortly afterwards, one fellow turned up at Granada's Manchester studios, blacked-up and dressed as an Indian, and calling himself Sheik Doud Ismael.

His 'disguise' didn't fool the TV production team, however. The comedian – who turned out to be a 40-year-old father-of-four from Norfolk – was given an audition, along with others. He was funny, but not apparently funny enough!

'The most important thing in choosing the comedians for the show,' says Hamp, 'is their faces. The face must be "different". Then comes delivery and timing. And thirdly, the joke itself. In that order.'

The Comedians are totally and unashamedly outrageous in all that they do. This is why they have succeeded. Nothing, or no one, apparently, is sacred. And their jokes prove it. They joke about nothing and everything. Anyone and everyone. They joke about false teeth and parrots and homosexuals virtually in the same breath. They joke about Catholics and Protestants. They joke about Pakistanis, the Irish and the Jews. They joke about Enoch Powell, the Queen and the Pope.

When they go out in front of the cameras, it is invariably a no-holds-barred encounter with the British viewing public. You either take it . . . or switch over to another channel. Viewing figures have already conclusively proved that viewers, who are always the final judges in these things, stay tuned in.

Since the show shot to the top, and scored consistently in the TV audience ratings, it has created untold jealousy not only in the BBC camp but also among the ranks of the well-established top-name TV comedians. It has also completely re-shaped the lives of some of those once-struggling funny-men now involved in the programme.

Ken Goodwin quickly found himself on the stage of the London Palladium in the 1971 Royal Variety Show, in front of the Queen and the Royal Family.

He has also branched out into the recording field, has cut an LP as a vocalist, and had his own TV Special. He was voted top comedian of 1971 by *The Stage* newspaper, and came second in a poll among *TV Times* readers, for the Funniest Man on television. Benny Hill was at number-one!

Bernard Manning, too, now has a recording contract as a straight singer. Frank Carson was featured in the BBC-2 programme *One Man's Week*, which was very good for prestige value, and George Roper, Steve Faye and Mike Burton were all chosen to appear before the Queen in a special Liverpool Royal show, at the Empire Theatre, in June 1971.

The Comedians was voted the best comedy show of 1971 by the TV Critics Circle, and by the theatrical trade paper *The Stage and Television Today*.

When a long-playing record was first issued by EMI of *The Comedians* TV show, the first 5,000 copies sold out within a week. More records were pressed, and a sale of more than 30,000 rapidly shot the LP into the best-selling charts.

The laughing boys have since spread their wings, and the TV show has been extended to the stage, with one company of comics going on tour and finishing up at Blackpool for the summer season of 1972, and another company achieving the top accolade of show business by appearing in a season at the London Palladium and in a Royal Gala Variety show.

The real secret of the success of *The Comedians* as a TV programme is simple. There is no top-of-the-bill, so that everyone has to work hard to make the programme 'come alive.'

Seeing it on screen, as a finished product, is deceptive. The TV programmes are actually recorded in lengthy two-and-a-half hour sessions, with each comedian doing a stand-up spot of 15 or 20 minutes.

Then the tapes are cut up, the jokes ruthlessly edited, chopping them down to size. Some comedians are cut out altogether. Others stay in. From these tapes, Johnnie Hamp and Wally Butler make up a series of half-hour shows.

The studio audiences are important. 'We like them to come in coach-loads, parties of women from clubs or factories, all on a night out and determined to have a good time,' says Hamp. There is a simple reason for this. People laugh more readily and heartily when they are sitting next to someone they know.

17

Music, too, is all important to the show's success. 'We wanted some lively music, and we brought in Shep's Banjo Boys as the resident group because they play the kind of music that automatically makes the audience want to tap their feet and clap, and this puts everyone in a happy frame of mind before we start the tapes rolling.'

The studio audiences are 'warmed up' by one or two of the comics themselves. Some of the lads are often tempted to throw in the occasional slightly risqué joke, if ever the audience shows the slightest sign of slackening up on the laughs. But they do this knowing only too well that any 'blue' ones are certain to be cut out.

This may be a tough, indelicate joke programme. But it's not a dirty one!

Chapter Two
STEVE FAYE

IF EVER Steve Faye feels like a good laugh, he goes to the loo. Don't get the wrong idea – that is where he keeps most of his jokes.

He has his gags, hundreds of them, written on the backs of Tote betting tickets, and he keeps them stacked away in the WC. 'You can spend a very pleasant hour or two having a chortle in our loo any time,' he says with that Liverpudlian good humour which has made him so popular on the TV show.

Steve boasts that he's the only one from *The Comedians* who still lives in a council house. But this doesn't seem to worry him in the slightest. There is none of the big-star bit about Stevie, anyway.

He was born in the rough, tough Dingle area of Liverpool of a very big family . . . 'I think my mother had about 12 of us'. He hesitates as though he has to think about it. His father was a docker. And that's where Steve derived his sense of humour.

'The Liverpool dockers are so funny. They're the finest unpaid comics in the whole world,' he insists. 'No one needs a scriptwriter when you can talk every day of the week to the dockers. All the dockers have got nicknames for each other.'

Like . . .

'The Amateur Boxer' – he sits in the corner with his gloves on.

'The Broken Boomerang' – he goes home for his dinner, but never comes back.

'The Prince of Wales' – when he's finished, he's in the Queen's Arms.

'Docker Dolittle' – he's so lazy, he won't do a tap all day.

Steve himself has never worked as a docker, but he drinks regularly with them. And it's from the dock workers that he picks up a lot of his comedy material.

For 16 years, he worked for British Railways, as a driver. Then he was given his cards – because he was always trying to be funny.

He's been described – even by other comics – as the funniest man in Liverpool. Which is quite a claim.

Yet it was only by accident that he became a full-time entertainer. He was quite happy, working for the Railways. ('You don't work on the railways – you just clock on and clock off'). Until one night when he got up to tell a few jokes in a pub.

A comedian called Bobby Shack heard him, recommended him to the Merseyside Artists Association, and Steve was offered his first booking. A booker for the Ford motor company said, 'I'll give you seven quid for a night.' Steve was flabbergasted at such money. 'Seven quid?' he queried. He must have sounded insulted, because the fellow quickly said, 'All right. Nine!' Steve jumped at the offer. He was earning only £11 a week on the railways, and the thought of £9 for one night's joke-telling more than appealed to him. This led to more regular bookings, as a part timer.

His first attempt at TV was an appearance in Hughie Green's *Opportunity Knocks*, in 1966. 'That led to really great things,' cracks Steve, 'Six weeks on the ovens at Jacobs biscuit factory, and a charity show in Vietnam.'

The Railways finally gave him his cards, when he took time off to do a tour overseas – and reported back a week late. ('They had been complaining for some time about my entertaining activities'). So this decided him to turn full-time comedian.

'I now drop the Railways a postcard every year, thanking them for doing me the favour of sacking me,' he says.

Steve has tried his hand at all kinds of jobs in his time. Cook, apprentice chef, hotel porter, lorry-driver. He was in an RAF fire crew. He worked in a candle factory – but got all the in-

20

gredients mixed up and sent everyone slipping and sliding on candle grease.

'I also worked in a glue factory – but I couldn't stick it.'

Once, working in a barber's shop, he bought half a dozen 'razzers' from a joke shop, and put them under the seat cushions. When the customers came in on a busy Friday night, the chairs made rude noises every time anyone sat down.

The barber pointed him to the door, and said, 'Go and get your coat, and go home. Your cards will be posted to you on Monday.'

Steve Faye would do anything for a laugh. Anything. Once, at large in Doncaster with Irish comedian Bal Moane, he pretended he'd been bitten by a dummy guide-dog-for-the-blind outside a chemist shop. A woman screamed when she saw Steve's half finger, a crowd gathered, the manager of the shop protested, but eventually took the dog in – 'So that it causes no more trouble'. Then the police arrived.

To avoid arrest, Steve pretended they were from *Candid Camera*. The hilarious incident ended with the shop-manager giving Steve a bag full of toothbrushes, etcetera, and wanting to know when he would be appearing on *Candid Camera*. Steve and Bal Moane fled before the policeman got wise to their antics.

'It is often very difficult trying to keep a job down when you're a natural comic,' says Steve. 'Bosses don't like people who like a laugh . . . I've been fired from more places than Soft Joe simply because the bosses always thought I was acting the fool.'

Life has been full of ups and downs for Steve. Especially when he worked as a lift attendant. One man consistently smoked a pipe in the little lift. So one day, Steve, only 16, picked up a bucket of water which was kept in the lift for emergency fire-fighting operations, and threw it over the man's pipe.

The boss fired him for that. But Steve had the nerve to ask for a reference so that he could get another job. 'A reference?' asked the boss. 'Yes,' said Steve. 'But I'll promise not to get another job as a lift-boy, or ever to set foot in this building.'

In his younger days, he was interested in football and boxing. 'I did a bit of amateur boxing myself. I wasn't very good, though. I was the only boxer in Liverpool who had adverts on the soles of my boots.

'They always knew I'd be a funny boy, 'cos even when I first came into the world, I was the only baby who laughed when they slapped me!'

21

Steve is a non-stop, 24-hour-a-day comic. He sometimes arrives home at 3 o'clock in the morning, and wakes up his wife Mary to tell her a new joke he's heard. (That usually goes down very well and does a lot to cement marital relations!)

He's been married 20 years, and has two children. 'Susan is eight, and Stephen is 18. He'd have been 20, but me and the wife were both a bit shy.'

Another of his favourite pastimes is stopping to give lifts to people in his car. Then, dead-pan, he will unexpectedly reach for a microphone under the dashboard and say: 'I've just picked up a fare.' 'I love looking at the surprise on passengers' faces when I do this,' chuckles Steve.

Steve will never work 'blue' material in his act. He once travelled to Birmingham to play a club, and found he was expected to go on at 11 o'clock after three strip-tease girls. 'Forget it,' he said to the manager, 'I don't do that sort of stuff.' And he walked out, amid fierce protestations.

'I just can't do "blue" stuff,' he says. 'I'll slip in the occasional naughty one, but I won't do any "stag" shows. It's just filth they want.

'Mind you, I've played some tough places. There's one pub I know that's so tough, even the manager's dog is a boxer.'

He much prefers the clean stuff. Little jokes which he builds up into full routines . . .

'Where's that feller who sold me a wrist watch?'
'Somebody put the finger on him, and he got time. The Judge ticked him off. He was going to give him six months, but he wound up giving him 12. He'll be out in the Spring.'

'I never do material which other comics are doing,' says Steve. 'I've always tried to be original.' He used to dress up in a tramp's outfit for his act. 'The trouble was, no one ever recognised me.'

Ken Dodd advised him to forget the tramp's outfit, and go on stage as himself.

Steve wore the tramp's get-up – a wig, false nose, glasses, a funny hat and a long coat – when he appeared last year on the Royal Gala show, attended by the Queen at the Liverpool Empire theatre.

After the show, he was introduced to the Queen. But ask Steve what Her Majesty said to him, and he'll reply: 'She said, "Hey, Steve, are you still using Yates's Wine Lodge these days?"'

He's got an infectious chuckle. 'When I'm out on stage, I'm in another world completely,' he says. 'I just love seeing people laughing and enjoying themselves.'

It's not always plain sailing, however. More than once, he's been attacked on stage by night club patrons who took objection to some of his jokes.

'I used to tell a few jokes about prison life'.

('They've got a smashing football team at Walton Jail. But the only trouble is, the Governor won't let them play away from home').

'I was playing a club in Brighouse, Yorkshire, when a bloke jumps up on stage and says: "Hey, I used to be in the nick." He was a big feller, so I had to joke my way out of it. I said, "Ladies and gentlemen, this man has been in the nick, and he wants us all to know about it.

"Was it GBH, grievous bodily harm? Or breaking into piggy banks? Has anyone in the audience got any questions to ask this gentleman about life in the nick?"'

But, more seriously, he feels that comics should have greater protection when they are on stage. 'In some clubs, that fellow would never have got near the stage . . . they'd have bounced him out.'

Steve is a verbal joke-machine. He knows how to handle an audience, even the awkward customers. Once he said to a young fellow who kept standing up, 'All right, son, sit down. We've all seen the suit.' The bloke replied, 'Yeah, and it's paid for.' 'I'm not surprised,' quipped Steve, 'You've been up and down so much, you've not put your hand in your pocket to get a round of drinks in yet.'

The chap's mates roared hysterically with delight. After that, Steve could do no wrong.

'There's always one clever fellow in every audience who tries to show you up,' he says. 'You've got to show that you are faster with words than he is.'

When he turned up at one club in Manchester, the manager said, 'I want you to do four spots tonight.' Steve said, 'Four?' The fellow said, 'Why, can you do more?' Steve replied, 'Well, I used to have a dozen spots, but I rubbed that Valderma in, so now I only have two.'

Life with the Fayes is full of fun. A neighbour once knocked on the door of the Faye household, rolled up his trousers to show a nasty bite, and complained: 'Your dog went for me last night.' Steve chortled: 'Well, you were ruddy lucky. When ever I send him for an *Echo*, he won't go for me.'

(Heard the one about the dog who used to dig holes in people's gardens? The neighbours were not amused. The trouble was, his previous owners had emigrated to Australia . . .)

Stopped for speeding, in Barnsley, he was told by a policeman he was doing 42 mph, in a radar beam. Steve laughed and said, 'Will you put that in writing. My mechanic will be tickled pink when I tell him. I've never had more than 28 mph out of this old banger before.'

As a driver with British Railways, Steve's official BR car once broke down – so he ended up taking two high-ranking Railway officials from Liverpool to Ditton Junction in an ice-cream van he'd borrowed in a hurry from a friend.

'I couldn't stop the bell ringing as we went along, and I had to keep stopping to serve ice-creams to children and housewives who came running, screaming after the van,' he chuckles. 'It ended with my two passengers, the big nobs from the Railways, both sucking a free ice-cream cornet apiece.'

He had a lot of fun with BR. ('Well, they're all jokers themselves on the Railways. One time, I remember, they built a lovely new signal-box . . . then had to knock it down because it was built on the wrong side of the track.')

'Even my mother is funny, although she doesn't realise it,' says Steve. 'Not so long ago, someone stopped her in the street and said, "Are you a native of Liverpool?" My mother said, "Am I hell! I was born here!"'

———————————

Heard about the fellow who booked to go on a holiday abroad. He told his mate he was paying for it on HP.
'Why?' asked his pal.
'Cos if the plane crashes on the way back, I'll get a free holiday.'

A fellow went to the doctor, and said, 'Doctor, I think I'm going insane.'
The doctor said, 'I know just how you feel . . . isn't it maddening?'

The woman who went to the psychiatrist and said, 'I've come about my husband, he thinks he's a rabbit.'
The psychiatrist said, 'Well you'd better tell him to buck up.'

An old woman went into the butcher's shop and said, 'Have you got a sheep's head?'
The butcher said, 'No, it's the way I part my hair.'

A fellow was walking down the street when he found a wage packet.
He pocketed the money, and his mate said, 'You're dead lucky, you are.'
The first fellow said, 'Lucky? You must be joking. Just look at the tax I've paid!'

A docker came out of the dock gates in Liverpool. The policeman on the gate said, 'Come here, what have you got on you?'
He said, 'Nothing', and then ran down the road. The policeman went after him, caught him 50 yards down the road and brought him down with a lovely rugby tackle. Then he searched him, and the policeman said, 'You've got nothing on you.'
The docker said, 'I told you I had nothing.'
Policeman: 'Well, why were you running away?'
Docker: 'I was just timing you for tomorrow night.'

An Inspector gets on the bus, goes up to the top deck. 'Tickets please?' He looks at one fellow's ticket and says, 'Where did you get on?'
He says: 'Downstairs, stupid!'

I love the odd names they have for the Dockers in Liverpool . . .
One fellow was called The Poet. He said, 'This job is just like Heaven – I haven't done a tap since half-eleven.'
The boss heard him, and he said, 'Hickory, dickory, dock – you can pick up your cards at five o'clock.'

A fellow went to the bank and asked for a loan. The bank clerk said, 'I'm terribly sorry, but the Loan Arranger isn't in.'
He said, 'Well, who do I see?'
The clerk said, 'Tonto.'

Two monkeys in a cage. One said, 'I'm starving.'
The other said, 'Well, there's plenty of bread. Why don't you make some toast?'
He said, 'How can I make toast in here?'
The other one said, 'Stick it under the gorilla.'

A young girl in a mini skirt gets on the bus. Two old men are sitting opposite her, both looking at her legs. One says to the other: 'Jimmy, remember the First World War?'

Jimmy says, 'I do, I do.'

He says: 'Remember those pills they used to give us to stop us worrying about sex?'

Jimmy: 'Yes, I do.'

He says: 'Well, I think mine are wearing off.'

I got myself a job as an AA man in a holiday camp last year. I had to go into the chalets at night, and say, 'Eh, eh, you can't do that! Eh, eh, cut that out!'

Two geese in a farmyard. One says to the other, 'What do you do whenever you feel lonely?'

The other one said, 'Oh, I just have a gander around.'

A fellow in the Army lost his rifle. The Sergeant said, 'You'll have to pay for it.'

He said, 'What! Pay for it? That's ridiculous. What would you do if I lost a tank?'

The Sergeant said, 'You'd have to pay for it, just the same.'

He said, 'Blimey! No wonder, in the Navy, the Captains go down with their ships.'

A fellow went to the Psychiatrist and said, 'I'm a bit worried. I keep thinking I'm a horse.'

The psychiatrist said, 'Well, I think I can cure you. But it will cost a lot of money.'

The fellow said, 'Money is no object. I've just won the Grand National.'

This fellow in the pub said to another bloke: 'Do you always drink your whisky neat?'

He said, 'No, sometimes I drink with no tie on, and my shirt hanging out.'

A fellow went to the pet shop and said he wanted a dog to catch the rats. He got one, took it home. Next day, he was back in the shop.

He said, 'I thought you said this dog was a good ratter? Last night, a couple of rats came out of a hole under the skirting board, ran right in front of the dog's nose, and he didn't do a thing about it.'

The shop-keeper said, 'Yes, well they're your own . . . Just wait till any strange rats come in the house.'

A fellow came up to me in the pub and said, 'Do you want to buy a leopard skin coat for your wife?'
I said, 'What's it like?'
He said, 'It's absolutely spotless.'

This fellow came up to me in Liverpool and said, 'Where's the nearest boozer?'
I said, 'You're talking to him.'

A road sweeper went to see the boss, and complained: 'I've had just about enough. You're always moaning "Brush this road; brush that road." I'm going crackers, you're working me too hard. I've got too many roads to brush.'
The foreman said, 'O.K., go home, get a good night's sleep, and tomorrow we'll give you only two roads to brush.'
He said, 'Fine. Which roads?'
Foreman: 'The M1 and the M6.'

A bloke was in the Army, posted abroad. And he got a letter from his wife, telling him she'd just had a baby.
He said, 'I'm going to celebrate tonight, I've just become a father.'
His mate said, 'Hang on, how can that be? You've been stationed out here for three years and you've not been home.'
He said, 'So what? Three years isn't much. There's five years between me and my brother.'

A motorist was stopped by a policeman for drunken driving. He insisted he should have an alcohol test, and handed him a balloon, saying 'Blow this up.'
The drunk said, 'Who's in goal?'

Chapter Three
KEN GOODWIN

KEN GOODWIN once travelled all the way from Crewe to London by row-boat in the guard's van of a train.

Crazy? Of course it is. But that's Ken. Anything for a laugh. Any time. Any place. 'All kinds of silly things keep happening to me,' he says with that childish chuckle now so familiar to TV audiences.

The trip by 'boat' from Crewe to London happened when Ken turned up at the railway station, complete with his rowing machine which he uses to help keep his weight down. But there wasn't a single seat on the train . . . so he ended up in the guard's van, sitting in his rowing contraption.

Goodwin has emerged from *The Comedians* as one of the brightest stars on the British comedy scene.

Born in Manchester, he came from a poor, working-class family. ('We were so poor that my Mam used to send me to the butcher's shop to buy a sheep's head, and she'd say, "Don't forget to ask him to leave the legs on."')

His father died when Ken was quite young, and the family hit on hard times. 'I used to deliver papers, as a nipper, and I recall one kind lady giving me a pair of trousers because mine had a few holes in them. They were lovely check trousers. When I went home and put them on, I thought it was Whit Week.'

He started playing the ukelele, and his big brother Jim, who became head of the family, encouraged Ken to take proper music lessons. His real ambition, however, was to be a footballer, not an entertainer. He used to run five miles every night in order to keep fit, and was even offered a trial with Manchester City – as a goalkeeper.

(Joe Mercer, manager of Manchester City: 'Ken Goodwin as a goal-keeper? It certainly makes me laugh!')

But he was standing underneath a goalpost when it collapsed and fell on top of him, and he severely injured a hand. ('It was the worst hand I've ever had – and I don't want another like it.')

Doctors told him he would never play the ukelele again – or play goalkeeper.

'If anything is going to happen to anyone, you can be sure it will happen to Ken,' says his wife Pat cheerily.

Odd things happen easily to Goodwin. In the Army, he once knocked down a telegraph pole when he lost control while driving a tank.

On another occasion, he was rush-marched into the CO's office. 'Left, right, left, right, left, right. Halt!' Ken came abruptly to attention and saluted . . . but he accidentally slid across the highly-polished floor and his knee knocked the desk, spilling the inkwell all over the CO's papers. 'I didn't know whether to laugh or cry,' recalls Ken. The CO, however, was not amused.

Ken was clearly not destined to be a soldier. He tried his hand at several jobs. He worked as a door-to-door salesman, trying to sell encyclopaedias ('I never sold any but I learned a lot'). But he did manage to sell some cookery books, and these brought him in £10 a week in commission. ('I used to know how to cook an egg thirty five different ways').

He also worked as a coalman ('I was dirt cheap'), and a brewery drayman ('I was only in that for the beer').

This tall, gangling comic worked small-time club dates in between his various jobs – playing the banjo or ukelele and singing George Formby's old songs.

Ken is very thin. So thin, particularly a few years ago, that his fellow comics still joke about the time he went swimming at Blackpool. A man was throwing sticks into the sea for his dog to bring back. And the dog brought Ken back three times.

He's also shy. More so now than when he was younger. 'I first started entertaining by doing little bits at Sunday School concerts, but I was so nervous I got my words mixed up. And the audience used to laugh at me. The more muddled I got, the more they laughed.'

This was at St. Luke's, Newton Heath, Manchester. When he forgot what to say, he would stammer and fill in with 'er . . . er . . . er.' 'This kind of stammering got me my biggest laughs, so now I just put these pauses into my act,' he says. 'I'm not as nervous as I pretend to be.'

So this is how Ken developed his present style – through his own nervousness. It's the same when he laughs at his own jokes . . . even though he's heard most of them before! 'When I first started, I had to laugh – after all, I was the only one laughing.'

There is nothing coarse about his humour. His jokes come from kids' comics, books, and from his own children – 13-year-old Belinda and 11-year-old Mandy.

'My family seem to think I'm funny, and that helps a great deal,' he says. 'No comedian would dare tell the jokes I tell, until they've heard me getting laughs with them.'

In 1964, he won a £100 talent contest at Leek, Staffordshire, and this decided him to turn full-time professional.

Ken likes 'family' jokes. Especially about children.

A small boy gets on a bus and tries to travel free.
'How old are you?' asks the conductor.
'I'm four,' says the child.
'When will you be five?'
'When I get off the bus.'

'Those silly sort of jokes get all the Mums laughing,' says Ken. 'And as a family comic, that's what I want.'

He pops in lots of Lancashire humour whenever he can. A small egg is called 'a chucky egg', so he'll joke about having eggs chucked at him – 'chucky eggs, of course!'

On the first three TV tapings of *The Comedians*, Ken found himself going on last. He sat in the studio and heard all the other comics before him. 'I had my list of jokes. So every time I heard one of mine told, I had to cross it off. I was adding and subtracting all the time.'

Last Christmas, he played Simple Simon in a London panto-mime. Before that, he was a big hit on the 1971 Royal Variety Show at the London Palladium.

('When I walked in and asked where the Queen would be

sitting, someone said "She'll have her own Royal box". I said, "Wouldn't you think they'd give her a proper seat?")

After the show, he met the Queen and other members of the Royal family. 'The Queen came up to me, shook my hand and said, "Very enjoyable. Where are you working next week?" I said, "Bristol." She said, "Very good," and she went. Then Princess Anne came up to me, shook my hand and said, "Very enjoyable. Where are you working next week?" I said, "Your Mam's just asked me that."'

Ken was a stranger to London until he made his debut at the Palladium. ('It was awful trying to get digs in London. I knocked on the door of one boarding house, a woman opened it, and I said, "I'd like to stay here." So she said, "Well, stay there" – and closed the door on me.')

He's got a natural, built-in grin. He finds that his teeth help to give him this. In fact, he's looking forward to one day meeting Ted Heath . . . so they can shake teeth!

One thing Ken has always worried about is his appearance. He likes to stay slim, and look fairly well groomed.

('Once, I was putting some toilet water on my hair – and the seat fell down and hit me on the head.')

Audiences love him because he's so innocently stupid. He gags: 'Don't make a noise – I've got a headache.' And will follow this up with: 'I'm too good for this place, aren't I?', which has now become his well-worn catch-phrase.

When he is bored, he tells them so. 'I'm going now, because I get fed up after a bit.' This line always guarantees a laugh.

Having now branched out as a singer, too, Ken is determined to prove himself an all-round entertainer. He made his first LP record, *Settle Down With Ken Goodwin*, and Granada crowned off 1971 for him with a special TV show, *Ken Goodwin's Golden Year*.

And who'd argue with that?

––––––––––––––

Judge: 'Why did you shoot your husband with a bow and arrow?'
Woman in dock: 'Because I didn't want to wake up the children.'

An Irishman telephoned the airport and asked, 'How long does

it take to fly to Ireland?'
The receptionist said, 'Just a minute.'
He said, 'Thank you very much', and put down the phone.

A plastic surgeon dozed off in front of the fire ... and he melted!

I went into a shop for a box of matches. I said, 'Are they British?' The lady behind the counter said, 'Yes, every one's a striker.'

I took the dog for a walk the other day. A neighbour said, 'Why's your dog wearing brown boots?' I said, 'Because his black ones are in the menders.'

This little lad went dashing into the house and said, 'Mam, I've knocked the ladder down outside.'
His mother said, 'Well, don't bother me, go and tell your dad.'
The lad said, 'He already knows – he's hanging off the roof.'

A fellow went to the Doctor, and said, 'Doctor, I'm very worried. I keep thinking I'm a packet of biscuits.'
Doctor: 'A packet of biscuits? Those little square ones?'
He said, 'Yes.'
Doctor: 'With lots of little holes in?'
He said, 'Yes.'
The doctor said, 'Then you must be crackers.'

I went into a shop and I said, 'Do you sell sand?'
The assistant said, 'Yes. Do you want a big bag or a little bag?'
I said, 'You'd better give me a big bag. 'Cos I've just won a camel in a raffle.'

I stopped my car, and there was a policeman on the edge of the pavement, looking very angry.
He said, 'You can't park here.'
I said, 'Why?'
He said, 'Because you're on my foot.'
Then he said, 'You're in a one-way street as well.'
I said, 'Well, I'm only going one way!'

A chap went into the Opticians. The Optician said, 'Do you wear glasses?'
He said, 'Only when I want to see.'

I saw my mate in the street. I said, 'Where are you going?'
He said, 'I'm just taking my wife to the Doctor's. I don't like the look of her.'
I said, 'Well hang on, mate, I'll go home and get mine – I can't stand the sight of her.'

A little boy asked: 'Dad, how did I get here?'
His Dad, thinking quickly, said, 'I put this seed in the garden – and that's how it happened. You just grew.'
So the boy went out, bought a packet of seeds, and sprinkled them all around the garden. Next day, he went out, lifted up a big stone and saw a little frog.
He said, 'Well, you might be ugly, but I still love you . . . 'cos I'm your Dad.'

I got on a bus in Blackpool the other day, and I said to the conductor, 'Do you stop at the Imperial?'
He said, 'What – on my money?'

I was in a doctor's waiting room. And this little lad was sitting next to me, and he kept sniffing all the time. Oh, he did annoy me. So finally, I turned to him and said, 'Hey, have you got a hankie?'
He said, 'Yes, but I don't like lending it out to strangers.'

Chapter Four
FRANK CARSON

FRANK CARSON is a man who loves to listen to his own voice. 'I can out-talk anyone, anywhere,' he claims, without even making it sound like a boast.

'I can just go on talking, until I say something funny. It always comes. I never dry up. I just get verbal diarrhoea.'

Now, since his face has become so familiar, if he sees someone in the street or a bar looking at him, wondering where they've seen him before, he will go over to them and say, 'I'm Frank Carson. Don't you think I'm much more handsome off the screen than on it?'

He chuckles loudly at his own cheek. It's really all a lot of Irish blarney, of course. And he loves the reputation he has got. 'The Irish are loved all over the world,' he says proudly. 'Why? Because we have the ability to laugh at ourselves, no matter what . . .'

I met one of these Aborigine fellows, who was carving out different figures from a piece of wood. I said, 'Pardon me, what are those statues?'

He said: 'One's an Englishman, one's a Welshman, and one's a

Scotsman.'

I said: 'Why didn't you carve an Irishman?'

He said, 'I couldn't find a piece of wood thick enough!'

'Ah, it's the way I tell 'em . . .' (This has become his favourite catch-phrase.)

Frank was born on the poorer side of Belfast, near the docks. 'We lived only 300 yards from the Labour Exchange . . . my father was too lazy to walk very far,' he jokes. 'There were five in our family, but food was put on the table for four. The last one in, missed out. And when you went and reached over the table for food, you did it with a fork in your hand, as a means of protection.'

His father worked, he remembers, mainly as a bill-poster for a group of cinemas. 'He used to get up at four o'clock every morning to go out and post bills over someone else's. Then someone would post bills over his. And so it went on all day. Yes, they were troublesome times in ould Ireland.'

Frank was always a cheeky boy, daring to do something different. When he was barely ten he was up on stage as the cocky comedian with a minstrel group, doing charity shows organised by the priests. He was then known as 'Snowball' Carson because of his beautiful flaxen hair.

He worked in a bookshop from the age of 12, earning seven-bob a week, after school.

'A woman came in one day and asked, "Have you got 'The Life of a Saint?"' I said, "Listen, missus, I haven't got the life of a dog in 'ere!"'.

At 14, he left school and got a job as an apprentice electrician. But not for long . . . He was digging a hole outside a house, put his pick through an electric cable – and fused the whole North side of Belfast for three days!

After that he worked as a plasterer, carrying cement ('I really got stuck into that job'), and then went into the Paratroopers for three years, and served in the Middle East.

He still doesn't know whether there was a war on or not at the time. And if so, which side he was on. On his demob, he turned full-time professional entertainer.

At one stage, he ran a public house. 'I'm the most easy-going and mild-mannered man in the world, and I never lose my temper. The only time in my life when I did,' he recalls, 'was when a bloke hurled a brick through my window. Next day he came back and threw another brick at me. But he missed. And I

36

threw it back at him – and hit him. I broke his jaw.

'The court case was funny . . . The judge said, "During the melee, were you cool, calm and collected?" I said, "I was cool and calm alright, but it was him who did the collecting!"'

He first met John Hamp in a tiny place called Ballyshannon. Hamp, then manager of the Metropole, Edgware Road, was looking for Irish acts and went to see a summer season, at which Frank was taking the tickets at the door as well as being on stage.

'I was told Mr. Hamp was an impresario from London, so I threw in half-a-dozen of my best gags. He didn't laugh at one of them,' recalls Frank.

'The show was in a theatre with a corrugated roof. If it rained – which was fairly frequent in Ireland in the summer – the band played, because the audience couldn't hear anyone speak on stage for the sound of the rain on the roof.'

Frank did hundreds of radio and TV shows in Ireland before moving to England, six years ago. He made appearances on the BBC's *Good Old Days*, then 'flopped', he admits, on the Cilla Black TV show. He did summer seasons at Butlins and Pontins holiday camps, and a TV series with The Bachelors. But it was *The Comedians* in which he really made a giant impact.

'Yet when Johnnie Hamp first told me he was going to do a show with a group of stand-up comedians, I told him straight the programme would die on its arse,' he says. Fortunately for Frank, he was wrong.

The first thing he said when he walked on the TV set for *The Comedians* was: 'Would you turn off some of those lights? You're going to fade this suit.' Then . . . 'Is there anyone in from Northern Ireland?' Someone in the audience said, 'Yes'. Frank cracked: 'Well, you'd better get home, your house is on fire.' It earned him a big laugh.

After that, he just couldn't put a foot, or a word, wrong. Immediately after the show, Hamp said simply, 'Knock-out . . . you're booked for the next seven shows.'

'I've never been paid off, as a comedian, in my life,' is one of Frank's proud boasts. 'Mind you, there are some pretty tough clubs up in Sunderland. There, the customers play draughts with manhole-covers, and the first four acts are usually eaten for supper by the club social secretary.'

But he insists: 'If an audience doesn't get your stuff, the answer is – change your material. If you cannot make an audience laugh, it's not their fault . . . it's yours!'

His father is a very funny man, says Frank with great affection. 'We were driving past Bangor, where there is a massive oil refinery. It was all lit up, with a thousand pipes towering up into the sky. I said to my father, "What a fantastic technological achievement that is, eh?" He sat back in the car, puffed on his pipe, and replied: "Ugh, rubbish! I could have told 'em there was oil there forty years ago."'

On another occasion, his father was telling Frank's daughter Majella about the First World War. 'I lost three quarter of a million of my mates,' he said. 'The enemy shelled us for 29 days morning, noon and night. We was up to our knees in water for 29 days.' Frank interrupted: 'Dad, that must have been rough?' 'Rough?' came the reply. 'Rough? I don't know how I slept through it all.'

Frank is married, with three children – a daughter and two sons, now all in their teens. He settled in Blackpool. 'The first house I bought was too small, and the second house I bought was too big.' Somehow, quite by accident, Frank found himself occupying a large house with 16 bedrooms.

'It was a boarding-house, only we never had any boarders. Except free-staying ones. Most of my relatives from Ireland all came over for free holidays. The children would bring dozens of stray people home to stay the night. It seemed like hundreds of people just came and stopped. I didn't know most of them. But no one would ever wash the dishes . . . I finished up washing them myself. So we sold that house, and got out.'

He has a fantastic memory for jokes, and doesn't even need to write them down, like most other comedians. 'Even if I lost my legs, I'd still like to be pushed on in a chair so that I could go on telling gags,' says Frank.

'I've always been blessed with a face which, no matter what I do to it, never changes. It looks just the same in the morning as it does at any other time of the day. The only thing that can change it is plastic surgery.'

Which is a bit of Irish, if you like!

———————

They've just found a new way of cutting down on unemployment in Britain . . . They're going to raise the school-leaving age to 47!

The Pope has made a fortune out of his new book. It's called *The Pill's Grim Progress*.

They've just invented a new pill for Catholic women. It weighs three-and-a-half ton. You put it up against the bedroom door, and your husband can't get in.

Maggie Murphy went to the surgery. She said, 'Doctor, I've forgotten to take my contradictive Pills.'
The Doctor said, 'You're ignorant.'
She said, 'Yes, three months!'

I haven't spoken to my wife for eleven months . . . I didn't like to interrupt her!

My wife talks through her nose . . . Her mouth has worn out!

Mrs. Murphy was in the front row of the Church, when she accidentally fell, split the leg of her drawers, and went sprawling down the aisle, showing more than she should.
The priest said, 'If any man turns to look at that poor, unfortunate woman, may the Lord strike him blind.'
Reilly turned to Casey, in the second pew from the front, and said, 'I think I'll risk one eye.'

Two Irishmen. Murphy says: 'Do you want to buy a pair of boots. Seven and six?'
Flaherty says: 'All right', and gave him the money. He looks at the boots.
Flaherty: 'Wait a minute, these are odd boots.'
Murphy says: 'I know. That's a seven, and that's a six.'

Casey walked into a wake in Dublin. It was very dark and he'd had a few drinks already. And instead of looking into the coffin, he lifted up the lid of the piano. He took one look, and said: 'I don't know who he was, but by Gawd he had a marvellous set of teeth.'

I bought the wife a Jaguar for Christmas. It was very expensive but it was worth it. It bit her leg off.

I've received a letter from my Mother. She says: 'The insurance man called this morning, and said "If the last instalment on your Granny's funeral isn't paid, up she comes."'

39

'Your father has become a sex maniac and tries to make love to me every moment he gets . . . Please excuse the wobbly handwriting!'

'Your grandmother, who has been bedridden for 35 years, took a large dose of Epsom Salts yesterday. She came down the stairs for the first time today . . . The funeral was at three o'clock!'

'Your Uncle Joe drank a bottle of varnish by accident yesterday. He had a horrible death – but a lovely finish.'

'Your Uncle Paddy, who had been taking Liver salts for 37 years, died a fortnight ago. Yesterday, we had to go up to the cemetery and beat his liver to death with a stick.'

Sammy, who had two wooden legs, was fire-watching last night when the building went on fire. The fire brigade managed to save the building, but Sammy was burned to the ground . . . The insurance company wouldn't pay out, as they said he hadn't a leg to stand on.

Flanagan was dying. He called his closest friend, Murphy and he said, 'Listen Pat, we've been drinking together in the same boozer for 40 years. After I'm gone, every time you go in, have a drink for me. Promise!' And he passed on. So Murphy did this. Faithfully for two years, every time he went in the pub, he ordered two drinks. 'That's for Flanagan, and that's for me.' One day he went in and ordered only one Irish whiskey. The barman said, 'What's the matter? Have you forgotten Flanagan's dying wish?'
Paddy said, 'No. That whiskey is for Flanagan. But I'm on the wagon.'

News item in the paper: 'The body of a woman believed murdered 600 years ago was discovered by archaeologists in the Donegal Hills. The local Royal Ulster Constabulary are now looking for a 643-year-old man who may be able to help them with their inquiries.'

A fellow walked into a pub, and there was some nut-case shouting, 'Fools stand on the left, idiots on the right.'
This fellow said, 'I'm no fool.'
The bloke said, 'OK, stand on the right.'

A news report in today's paper: 'The East German pole-vaulting champion has just become the West German pole-vaulting champion.'

Officer Muldoon saw this tramp, Casey, walking down the street with a dog on the end of a piece of string. So he says to Casey: 'You need a licence for that dog. It will cost you 50 new pence, and you'd better report to the police station by tomorrow at 12 noon to prove you've got it.'
So next day, in walks Casey with a dog licence. Officer Muldoon was very suspicious. He said, 'Where did you get 50 pence from to buy a dog licence when you normally haven't got two pennies to rub together?'
Casey said, 'Oh, I sold the dog.'

In the USA. A black conductor suddenly pushed an old woman off the platform of the bus, for no reason at all. She died of her injuries, and he was sent to the electric chair.
Asked if he had any last requests, he said, 'Yes, I'd like a banana.' So they gave him a banana, he ate it. They pulled the switch, but nothing happened. So they had to release him.
Six months later, he went back to his old job. Saw another old lady, kicked her off the bus. Sentenced again to the electric chair. 'Any last requests?' 'Yes,' he said, 'I'd like a banana.' He ate it, they put him in the death chamber, pulled the switch. Nothing happened. He was on the way out, and the prison governor said to him, 'Tell me, how did you do it? Was it the bananas that saved you?'
He said, 'No, I was just a bad conductor.'

A fellow was walking past a Chinese restaurant. He saw a lot of rice on the pavement outside. He said to a fellow nearby: 'Has there been a wedding breakfast in there this morning?'
The chap said, 'No. Not at all. One of the customers has just knocked the stuffing out of the manager.'

One of the Irish labourers goes to see the foreman on a building site.
He says: 'Boss, the shovels haven't arrived. What shall we do?'
The foreman said, 'Tell the lads to lean on each other until they come.'

Chapter Five
COLIN CROMPTON

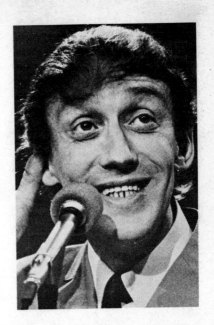

COLIN CROMPTON has made up his mind about one thing . . . he is definitely not going to Morecambe for his holidays this year. Or next.

He doesn't think much of Morecambe. At least, that's the impression he's given on *The Comedians*. Colin caused a storm of controversy in the Northern seaside resort last year when he bombarded – not to say slandered – the town with a string of anti-Morecambe jokes which would have run from one end of the promenade to the other.

In Morecambe, they don't bury their dead . . . they stand them up in bus shelters . . . with Bingo tickets in their hands!

I once spent 14 weeks in Morecambe. Well, somebody had to go there – and I lost the raffle. They put all the names in a hat, and Mr. Bernard Delfont pulls them out, and the one who loses has to go to Morecambe . . . It's like a cemetery with lights – Stockport, with sea.

If they want any excitement in Morecambe, they all go in the grocer's and watch the bacon-slicer . . . A lovely girl, she is!

Wednesday is the big day in Morecambe . . . everyone turns out

43

to watch the traffic lights change. Half-past ten, it is, if you don't want to miss it!

They dropped an Atom Bomb on Morecambe once. It did £15 worth of damage!

The ironic conclusion to this outburst was that he was later invited to Morecambe to switch on a set of autumn lights. But it wasn't the Corporation who invited him (they were furious). It was a businessman who felt that Colin, after all the bad but free publicity he'd given the town, should have been official 'switcher-on' of the town's lights, instead of actor Patrick Allen. Instead, Colin switched on the illuminations at a ballroom and bowling alley.

'It was all very funny,' says Colin impishly. 'I've got nothing really against Morecambe. It's just that I'd much prefer to spend one week there than two.'

Anyway, he prefers to go abroad for his holidays. 'Last year, we went to Spain – a little place called Costa Packet.

'A pal of mine likes those holiday camps. Y'know, the places where they have fellows in red blazers dashing around all day to make sure you enjoy yourself. And the same fellows dashing about all night to make sure you don't enjoy yourself!'

Colin has been 'discovered' so many times, he's lost count. 'Before *The Comedians* started, I was fed up with agents discovering me, promising to make me a star. That sort of thing gets a bit boring after the first 15 years.'

He's been a professional funny man, in fact, for 19 years. A bright lad, after leaving North Manchester Grammar School, he went to work in a bank. 'My father, who was in insurance, thought it was a respectable thing to do. It also meant security.'

Colin now laughs even at the memory of it all. His brother Neil is still in banking, and is a manager. 'I escaped,' says Colin smugly.

He worked in the bank for seven years. But then he started working, part-time, as a comedian. Northern radio producer Ronnie Taylor gave him an audition with the BBC, and Colin found himself being booked fairly regularly for radio programmes such as *Variety Fanfare*.

He fast proved himself a good comic. The only person who didn't laugh was his bank manager, who stiffly told Colin that banking was no laughing matter, and he'd better choose what he wanted to do in life. Colin surprised him – and his father – by quitting his job and turning full-time comic.

44

'I had nothing much to lose,' he recalls. 'The BBC were paying me seven guineas a broadcast, and I was earning only about £20 a month at the bank.'

But, just to show them, he kept his account at the same branch – and watched the bank manager's face go redder and redder over the years. ('I've since moved my account. I told them straight – I was taking my overdraft elsewhere.')

With no agent, Colin managed for a time to get most of his bookings himself. He toured for some years with revues, under such exotic titles as *Red, Hot and Blue*. Then, with the decline of variety theatres, he had to look to nightclubs for a living.

'Overnight, the theatres became super-markets. You went in to see a show, and they wouldn't let you out unless you had a wire basket'.

In his early days, Colin unashamedly modelled himself on both Ted Lune and Ken Platt. Later, however, he developed a more individual style of his own, and was a regularly in-work performer long before *The Comedians* shot him to TV fame.

('I've got a shocking cough. It's with getting out of a warm bed . . . to go home!')

He remembers one incident when he returned for a week at Leeds City Varieties Theatre, after a couple of years away. At band call, the violinist came up to him and said, 'Oh, I remember you. You're the fellow who always works with a cigarette in your hand.'

'That's right,' said Colin, quite flattered that the fellow should remember him. 'Yes,' said the musician, 'But do you think this week you could avoid flicking your ash all over the orchestra?'

'Orchestra? There was a violin, a piano and drums,' laughs Colin. 'So I went on stage and flicked ash in all directions.' Eventually the theatre boss Stanley Joseph came to him and said, 'Don't offend them, Colin. We can always get a new comic, but it's not so easy to get a new violinist.'

Colin still works with a cigarette in his hand. In fact, he uses the cigarette to time his act. 'I smoke only Stuyvesant, and one cigarette will burn for exactly 15 minutes if I don't smoke it,' he says. 'So I light a cigarette as I go on, and just use it as a 'prop'. When that's finished, I'll light another. After two cigarettes, I'll know I've done 30 minutes, so I'll finish my act and get off.'

He goes through 40 cigarettes a day – but some of them are never smoked. He admits though: 'If the audience is not very good, I'll sometimes take a few puffs on the cigarette, so I can get off sooner.'

Off-stage, he wears glasses all the time. But he takes them off when he is in front of a TV audience or on stage. ('I just can't bear to see people suffer!')

Colin is now a firm believer that 'life begins at 40.' He was 40 last year, just after he got his big TV break with *The Comedians*. His birthday coincided with a happy domestic event – his second marriage. His first marriage broke up after five years. 'My wife left me, leaving me with our two children,' says Colin. Consequently, he had to readjust his working schedule and travelling, so that he could always get home each night to see his children. Last December, he married his housekeeper, Carol, who was once a ballroom vocalist with a dance band.

'She's been marvellous not only for me but also for my daughters, Cheryl and Erica,' says Colin.

Since the success of the TV show, Colin has opened a fashion boutique for his wife. They've called it, appropriately enough, *The Comedian's Wife*.

He's never likely to run short of gags, he says. After the great Bud Flanagan died, his widow wanted to give all his joke books to a 'deserving, up-and-coming' comedian. Colin, through a recommendation from Bud's long-time comedy partner Chesney Allen, was lucky enough to get them.

'Mrs. Flanagan wouldn't even take payment for them,' he says. 'She just asked me to give £20 to a charity.' So he now has thousands of jokes. Some old, some new. Some clean, some blue.

'If you can laugh at some of the jokes I've got, you can juggle soot'.

But another source of great comedy to him is a real-life pal called Tommy, who has found his way into Colin's act over the last few years. 'He's a real Lancashire Andy Capp character. His name is Tommy Hassall, and he's got a rather biggish wife, 12 kids, and he drinks like a fish,' says Colin. 'I just exaggerate slightly when I tell jokes about Tommy.'

My friend Tommy has been married 22 years and he's got 22 kids. His wife's never heard of Horlicks.

He's the only fellow I know who pays Income Tax on his Family Allowance.

When Tommy wakes up in the morning, he's got to kneel up in bed before he can see if it's light or not.

'He loves me making jokes about him. His wife, too,' says Colin.

Which is just as well!

I went to a smashing party. It was my Granddad's 103rd birthday party. He wasn't there, though . . . He died when he was 39.

I always feel sorry for people who don't drink. Because when they wake up in the morning, that's the best they're going to feel all day . . .

In this restaurant, there was an Englishman, a Scotsman and a Jew. (There always is in jokes, isn't there? I think the Irishman was ill!). They had a nine-course meal, and the bill came to £42. The Scotsman said, 'I'll pay that.'
You probably saw the headlines in the papers next day: 'Jewish ventriloquist found dead in alley.'

At Morecambe, they have boat trips every day. You go out for a pleasure cruise, round Heysham Head. They don't come back though . . . They've never found anyone who wants to!

There are some very nice drives out from Morecambe, aren't there? Any road is a nice drive out from Morecambe.

I know a bloke who's got a car which doesn't use any petrol. How I know is, he told me he took a girl all the way home to Nottingham last night – for nothing!

I went swimming the other day. A girl got out of the swimming pool and gave the baths attendant a penny. I thought that was very honest of her . . . (You'd think she'd have left it there . . .)

A fellow went to the Doctor.
He said: 'Doctor, I keep having great pain from my wooden leg.'
The Doctor said: 'How can a wooden leg give you pain?'
He said: 'The wife keeps hitting me over the head with it.'

There was a big Civic dinner, and the main course was boiled ham.

The Rabbi was there, so he politely refused, and passed it on. There was an RC priest sitting next to him and he thought he'd have a bit of fun, so he said to the Rabbi: 'When is your lot going to drop this silly, old-fashioned rule about not eating ham?'

The Rabbi said: 'At your wedding reception.'

I went to see that musical on stage, 'Oh Calcutta!'
Y'know, I never realised there were so many Jewish actors around!

My mate's wife is getting so fat, she washed her nightdress the other day and hung it out on the line to dry . . . And a family of gipsies moved into it . . . with two horses!

'Why do negroes wear white gloves in the cinema?'
'I don't know. Why?'
'So they'll know when they've come to the end of their choc-ice.'

Heard the one about the fellow who went into a hotel, met a bird in the bar, and they went to Reception and signed in as Mr. and Mrs. Smith for the night. Next day, he came down after breakfast and was presented with a bill for £200. He complained: 'But I've only stayed one night.'

The manager said, 'Yes, sir, but your wife's been staying here for six weeks.'

The silly story about the fellow who won £150,000 on the Pools, and decided to buy a motor car for the first time. He fancied a Rolls Royce, but the man in the showroom said, 'You want to start with something smaller, sir. Like a Mini.'

So he went to another showroom, and asked for a Mini.

The manager said, 'You don't want a Mini if you've not driven before. Why don't you get a motor scooter?'

So he went for a motor scooter. The man in the showroom said, 'That's too powerful to start on. Why not try a bike?'

So he went to buy a bike. But the fellow in the shop said, 'If I were you I'd start with a hoop and stick.' So he went to Woolworths and bought a hoop and stick for four shillings.

Next day, the weather was nice, so he went for a run to Southport. He went bowling off to the seaside with his hoop and stick.

Halfway there, he pulled up at a transport cafe for a cup of tea, and parked his hoop and stick in the car-park.

When he came out, someone had pinched it. He went in to the manager and complained that someone had taken his hoop and stick.

The manager said, 'Well, look we don't want any trouble, how much did it cost you?'

He said, 'Four shillings.'

The manager said, 'Here, I'll give you the four shillings to cover your loss.'

The fellow said, 'That's not the point. How am I going to get home?'

You've got to get married. You can't go through life being happy!

My mate Tommy is so absent-minded, he's got to buy a loaf of bread to find out what day it is!

He's drinking heavily as usual, my mate Tommy. He went on a trip abroad, and he was the only one in the coach party who couldn't see anything wrong with the Tower of Pisa.

He supped so much booze on the boat coming back, they had to pay duty on him to get him back in the country.

Tommy's got so many empty beer bottles in his back garden, it's put nearly £200 on the value of the house.

Tommy's got a sister, Ethel, and she moved in with her husband and family from a little terraced house to a big block of flats. They were on the 40th floor. The first day, they sent the kids out onto the balcony to look down at the aeroplanes.

Her husband said, 'Ethel, this is our first real home, so I hope you'll be proud of it, and keep it clean.'

She said, 'I will, I'm houseproud.'

Ethel went out on Tuesday, and didn't come back until Friday.

Her husband said, 'Where have you been?'

She said, 'I've been cleaning the steps.'

A self-service cafe is like getting married ... You choose what you fancy. Then, when you see what your mate's got, you want some of that as well!

I went on a pub crawl with my mate Tommy. He was driving, and we stopped at this little pub in a village. Tommy said to the barman, 'Have you got a big black dog with a white collar in this village?'

The barman said, 'No, we haven't.'

Tommy said, 'Well, have you got a big black cat with a white collar?'

He said, 'No.'

Tommy looked at me through glazed eyes, and said, 'There you are – it was the vicar I ran over!'

A vicar ran out of petrol while driving his car down a country lane. He didn't know what to do because he had no petrol can, so he finally got a little kiddies' potty from the boot, which he'd had for a family outing. He walked to the nearest garage and got the potty filled with petrol. He came back and was pouring it into the tank, when a passing motorist shouted out: 'Hey vicar, you've got more faith than I have.'

Chapter Six
CHARLIE WILLIAMS

CHARLIE WILLIAMS wishes to make it quite clear that he has nothing personal against Mr. Enoch Powell when he refers to him as 'my friend Knocker'.

For in Yorkshire, anyone who is called Enoch automatically gets the nickname of 'Knocker'. 'It's true,' says Charlie, trying not to grin but his teeth won't let him. 'Just like, in Yorkshire, anyone with the surname of Clark is called 'Nobby'. And when I was a kid, anyone christened Charlie was quickly nicknamed 'Wag'. Some of my old school chums still call me Wag.'

Charlie is now the darling of the Yorkshire night-club circuit – thanks to his tremendous impact and success in *The Comedians*. He's dark-skinned ('Not black,' he jokes, 'but if you put the lights out, you won't see me'), has buck teeth, and a broad Yorkshire accent which he deliberately exaggerates on stage.

He has been a professional comedian only a couple of years and is one of the new breed of coloured comics who is breaking down racial barriers with his own peculiar brand of 'black comedy.'

There are lots of jokes about Enoch Powell in his act. 'But I've nothing personal against him,' he says. 'Just wait until we

51

take over in ten years' time, that's all.'

'When Enoch Powell or anyone else says 'Go home, black man', it means I've got a helluva long wait for a bus to Barnsley.'

For Charlie, 43, was born in Royston, near Barnsley. His mother was a Yorkshire woman, his father an immigrant from Barbados.

He worked down the pit, straight from school-leaving age. His parents split up, and Charlie was adopted by another family.

At 17, he signed as a semi-professional with Doncaster Rovers football club, and continued to work in the coal mines until he eventually got a first-team place.

Attacking forwards soon feared the hard-tackling of Charlie Williams, who was one of the toughest centre or wing halves in the area. He stayed with Doncaster Rovers for 12 years – from 1948 to 1960 – keeping his place in the first team for five years, before being transferred to Skegness Town, as a semi-pro.

In April, 1957, Charlie married a Yorkshire girl – and proved himself something of a comedian even on his wedding night when he somehow managed to get himself locked in the lavatory.

'The toilet lock was a bad 'un. I went in, banged the door, and couldn't get out again,' he recalls. He eventually had to be rescued.

After quitting professional football, however, Charlie encountered some pretty tough times. He was offered a well-paid job as a soccer trainer in Sydney, and was all set to emigrate to Australia. But he was finally refused entry because of his colour. This was a great disappointment to him.

He then knew what it was like to join the dole queues. One winter he shovelled snow for a few pounds a week, and also tried his hand as a window cleaner.

Buying a bucket and a ladder, he thought it was easy. He went into partnership with another chap, Jim Walker. But Walker recalls: 'As a window cleaner, Charlie made a fine comedian.'

Charlie once fell off his ladder whilst cleaning the upstairs bedroom windows of a house. 'There was a loud clatter and a bang, and I looks up, and there's Charlie on his way down,' says Walker. 'All he said, as he came down, was "Move that bloody bucket."'

His venture into night club entertaining started with Charlie singing Nat King Cole songs. Then he gradually started slipping in jokes between his songs, and found he could get more laughs for the jokes than he did applause for the songs. So he packed up singing, and just concentrated on telling gags.

A fellow went into a pub, ordered a pint of bitter. He took one mouthful, pulled an awful face, and said to the barman: 'Hey, this beer's funny.'

The barman said: 'Well, laugh at it!'

His wife Audrey encouraged him to turn professional comedian two years ago. They have two children, Melford, 14, and Beverley, 12.

He's an infectious comic. Like Ken Goodwin, Charlie starts most of the laughter himself.

'To be honest, I find that white people are often too sensitive,' he says. 'It's only those who question some of my "colour" jokes who are really prejudiced. These people still have a deep-down fear of the black man. And it's this fear I'm trying to help break down, by telling jokes about it.

'A lot of coloured people are in my audiences in the clubs, and they laugh as much as anyone. In fact, I believe in giving 'em some hammer. After all, we tell jokes about the Irish, the Scots, and the Jews. So why should the black man get away with it?'

Did you hear the one about the 40 Pakistanis living in one house in Bradford? There used to be 41, but one fellow went to the Labour Exchange and said he wanted to be a conductor ... so they nailed him to the chimney-stack!

He threatens his audiences ... "If you don't laugh, I'll bring my tribe in and we'll eat the lot of you."

'Laughter,' says Charlie, 'is a wonderful noise. I like to have happy, smiling people around me. I suppose this is part of my West Indian blood. I have a very free-and-easy attitude to life.

'When I go out on stage, I go out there to win. Just like I used to do in football. It's me against them, and I must win – otherwise I'm a disappointed man.'

———

I went over to Birmingham. What a lovely country that is. And I told them, I said: 'I'm your next King' ...

I went into a posh restaurant. The waitress said: 'Excuse me, young man, but we don't serve darkies here.'

I said, 'That's all right, luv. I don't eat 'em.'

We had a fellow round to dinner at our house the other night. He said: 'I don't like your mother-in-law.'
I said: 'Well, that's all right, just eat the chips and peas.'

Enoch Powell was sitting on the Magistrates bench in court. A little Pakistani was up in front of him. Enoch said: 'The charge is riding a bike without lights. I find you guilty. Fined £70.'
The Pakistani said: 'What? £70 just for riding a bike without lights?'
Enoch said: 'Yes, and it would have been £200 if it had been dark.'

I was talking to our Saviour, Enoch Powell. I said 'Knocker, come 'ere, cock.' I told him, 'There's too many of them blacks here!' Cos I were here first, y'see, and they're all spoiling it now for me.

A coloured man went into a pub with a pig under his arm. The barman said: 'Where did you get that swine?'
And the pig replied: 'I won him in a raffle.'

Enoch Powell went to Ted Heath and said: 'After I'm dead, I'd like you to get 300 Pakistanis, and I want them all to stamp on my grave.'
Mr. Heath said: 'Are you sure, Enoch?'
He said: 'I'm quite sure. In fact, 400, if you can round them up.'
Mr. Heath said: 'Fair enough. Where do you want to be buried?'
Enoch said: 'At sea.'

A poor little Pakistani bloke went for a job on a building site, but he was told by one of his mates that they only took on Irish labour. So he went to the foreman, who said: 'What's your name?'
This Pakki said: 'Patrick Finnegan, sir.'
The foreman said: 'Fair enough, start on Monday.'
He said: 'Thank you very much, sir'.
He was just walking away, feeling very pleased with himself, when the foreman shouted after him: 'Oh, before tha' starts work on Monday, wash tha' face, thar's a good Catholic!'

I walked into a billiard saloon . . . and I heard this fellow say: 'I'll pot the black'. So I got out, smartish!

Three blokes all died at the same time, and went up to the gates of Heaven. Two white fellows and one black one. They're met by Angel Gabriel who says: 'There's no discrimination here, but you all have to pass a spelling test before you can come in.'
He said to the first white bloke: 'Can you spell God?'
He said: 'G O D.'
Gabriel said: 'Smashing. Come inside.'
He said to the next white fellow: 'Can you spell Jesus?'
He said: 'Yes, J E S U S.'
Gabriel said: 'Lovely. Come inside'.
Then he turned to the black man, and said: 'Now, you'll find no discrimination in here whatsoever. Can you spell Chrysanthemum?'

Hear the one about the black fellow who went for a job on a building site? He said to the foreman: 'I'd like a job. I've got a wife and 14 kids.'
The foreman said: 'Fine. Can tha' do anything else?'

I was driving along a country road when I sees this feller on the side of the road. I stopped, and I saw that this bloke had three eyes, no arms, and only one leg. So I opened the door and said, 'Aye, aye, aye, you look harmless . . . hop in!'

A bloke was walking down the road when he sees a fellow throwing a stick into the water, and his dog is walking across the water, ever so daintily, and bringing back the stick.
This fellow stops and says: 'Eeh by gum, that's a reet clever little dog you've got there, old flower.'
The man says: 'You must be joking, mate. He can't even swim.'

These Pakistanis . . . isn't there a lot of 'em? They're coming over here on camels, oil slicks, anything they can get on . . .
Mind you, I'm all right. I'm safe. Once the darkies take over, I can go over onto their side.

A pal of mine went into hospital to have his leg off. The doctor came round to see him next day and said, 'How's the leg?'
Fred says: 'Tha' should know better than me. It was thee that took it off.'

What about those poor slaves, in the olden days. On those galley ships, where the slaves had to do all the rowing. The

55

Captain shouted: 'More speed'. So the slave-master went to work with his whip on their backs, to get more effort out of them. But Number 27 keeled over and died.

The Captain said: Right, whip them all.'

The Slave Master said, 'But one of 'em's just died.'

The Captain said: 'That's what I mean, you've got to have a whip-round when somebody dies!'

This old-age-pensioner had a visit from the vicar. Old Bill said: 'What are you collecting this time for, vicar?'

The vicar said: 'For the good Lord.'

Bill said: 'Then you'd better leave the box, vicar, I reckon I'll be seeing Him before thee.'

This Yorkshire lad won £200 on the horses, so he thought he'd live it up a bit and go off to London. So he went and had a reet good day of it. He had a gamble or two – and lost. A jar or two – and lost. A bird or two – and lost. Then he found he didn't even have the fare left to get the train home, or even enough to get a decent meal or a night's kip. So he went to Hyde Park to doss down. He couldn't get in, it was full of Hippies and Aussies. So he went to Trafalgar Square. All the benches were taken up with tramps. So he staggered along the River embankment until he came to Chelsea Bridge, and he thought, 'There's nothing left. I've no choice. I'll have to sleep here.'

Just then, a big Rolls Royce draws up and out steps a beautiful big blonde lady, dripping with pearls. She says: 'Would you like to come home with me?' So he jumps in beside her, and she takes him home to this lovely big penthouse flat.

She says: 'Would you like a drink?' He says, 'Aye, a pint of brown mixed.' But she gives him champagne.

Then she gives him a big meal, with caviar sandwiches and everything. And afterwards she says to him: 'Would you like a nice bath?' He nods and says, 'Aye, I wouldn't mind.'

So she prepares a bath for him, puts in lots of those smelly bath-cubes, and gives him a pair of lovely pyjamas, with monogrammed lapels and everything. Then she says: 'Are you ready for bed?' He says: 'Yes, wouldn't mind.' So she takes him to the bedroom and pulls back the sheets, and goes out.

Back she comes a few minutes later, wearing a beautiful black negligee, and she strolls over to the bed. Then she drops the negligee off onto the floor, and the little fellow closes his eyes –

he can't even look.

She says seductively, 'Come on then, move over'. And he did . . . and fell right into the Thames!

I went to a fairground, and went on the darts stall. They gave me three darts. I said, 'Nay, never mind the darts, give me a blow pipe.' Cos I'm right handy with that, tha' knows!

Anyway, I won every time. Cleared the stall, I did. They gave me sixteen plastic bags of goldfish. I said, 'Well, they look very nice. But aren't you going to fillet 'em?'

The Priests were playing the Rabbis at football. And the Rabbis won 34–nil. The Priests got together and they said, 'We'll have to have a return match. But we'll beat 'em next time – we'll sign up a new centre-forward . . . Father Eusebio.' So they did. And another game was fixed up.

After the match, one priest rings up the Monastery and he says, 'We lost, 2–1.'

The Priest in charge says, 'You're joking! Who scored for us?'

He said, 'Father Eusebio.'

'And who scored for them?'

He said, 'Rabbi Charlton and Rabbi Best.'

Chapter Seven
TOM O'CONNOR

KEN DODD once described fellow Liverpudlian Tom O'Connor as 'The Bar-room Philosopher'. And that's pretty apt. For that's just what Tom is . . . a quick-witted schoolteacher who saves up his jokes for telling in his spare time.

Tom is the odd man out in *The Comedians*. He is the only part-timer in the TV ranks. A teacher at St. Joan of Arc RC School, Bootle, during the day, and a comedian by night. Yet he somehow manages to balance the two careers remarkably well.

In fact, he did try his hand as a full-time entertainer. That was five years ago. His showbiz career lasted exactly six months, and ended in disaster with Tom, in tears on the phone to his wife Pat. He was stranded, without a penny, in South Wales, after his car broke down.

'It taught me a sharp lesson,' he says frankly. 'Now I'm happy to be a full-time teacher and a part-time comic.'

Nevertheless, he's a busy man, often working six or seven nights a week at clubs within reach of Merseyside. 'I have now settled for security rather than fame,' he says. 'And *The Comedians* gives me all the recognition I want, outside of Liverpool.'

Tom, 32, is a good talker with a good brain. His night-club act runs for an hour without a break. And he specialises in telling the sort of smart jokes that the man in the street always wishes he could tell.

'I work very fast. If they don't get the jokes, I expect them to laugh now, and think about them later,' he says.

He's another whose father is a docker. 'My dad's a quay foreman. They call him 'The Blister' – he only shows up when the work's done.

'There's another fellow on the docks, they call 'The Diesel Man' – because he's always putting things in his pocket and saying, "Dese'll fit me dad, and dese'll do for me."'

Tom won a scholarship to grammar school at 11, and went on to become a teacher. He now teaches 15-year-olds, and must rank as one of the most popular teachers ever to run a classroom. He promotes the *Tom O'Connor Road Show*, which is a group of school kids who travel around, putting on stage shows for charity. Already, they have raised thousands of pounds, and have now undertaken to provide cash annually for the upkeep of a home for handicapped children recently opened at St. Annes-on-Sea.

'Since we started running the Road Show, three years ago, we've not had a single window broken at the school,' says Tom proudly. And Bootle is a tough area. By tradition, it's said, even the bugs in Bootle wear clogs!

'The lads come into school and tell me lots of jokes which they get from their fathers on the docks. But the problem is that most of them are too "blue" for me to use.'

He first started entertaining while at teachers' training college in London. He staged revues and then teamed up as a double act, vocal and comedy, with Brennie McCormack, playing at clubs three nights a week for thirty-bob. He also used to sing, with a guitar, outside Liverpool football ground. ('The supporters were very generous if the Reds won, but unbearable if they lost').

Tom went solo. But it wasn't easy, or very funny, for he was still trying to do a double act. And he was the straight man!

Slowly he developed a style of his own, and built up his appeal in Merseyside clubs. He's now broken the box-office record at several nighteries, and has a big, enthusiastic following of admirers.

The night he was auditioned for *The Comedians*, he knew nothing about it. His agent, Billy Scott, told him he was doing a concert for old-age pensioners at the Broadway Club, Liverpool. What Tom did not know was that Johnnie Hamp was in the audience. And he was so impressed with Tom that he signed him up for TV on the spot.

Since becoming one of the stars of the TV show, Tom has wrestled for months with the problem of whether he should give up teaching and turn full-time comic. His big decision to stay on in teaching was cemented when he was made deputy headmaster at his school, only recently. He is a dedicated teacher, and although he enjoys entertaining people he feels he has all the financial security he wants. His wife, who comes from Keighley, Yorkshire, is also a teacher – at St. Winifred's infants, Bootle, only a stone's throw from Tom's school.

They have four children – Anne, 8, Stephen, 7, Frances, 6, and Helen, 2. ('I took a couple of years off. Needed the rest,' cracks Tom).

'I find that teaching is a great leveller. My school job helps me to keep both feet firmly on the ground. I can be appearing on TV one night. But next day, in class, one boy might say, "Me dad saw you on the telly last night, sir – he thought you were bum."'

'You can't get ideas above your station with this sort of thing happening. The kids are marvellous. They make me realise too that I'm only as good as my last lesson. I can't show any of the big-star temperament when they're around . . . they'd just take the mickey out of me. I can say I'm a pro only when I go and do my act in a club. That's what matters.

'All Liverpudlians have this marvellous sense of humour.'

A fellow went into a fish shop the other day, and said, 'Have you got a cod's head for the cat?'
The fellow behind the counter said, 'Why? Are you doing a transplant?'

'In Liverpool,' says Tom, 'we're all brilliant. We're very modest, too.'

He is not averse to throwing in the occasional Catholic joke. (Two nuns sitting upstairs on a bus. 'Fares please?' says the conductor. The Nuns say, 'We haven't got any money for our fare, but we'll give you our names and address. We're both Sisters of John The Baptist.' The Conductor goes downstairs, and then comes back again, smartish. 'You two – off' he yells. 'I've just realised – John The Baptist is dead.')

Tom studies comedy very closely. 'It took me two years to find out just what it was about me that made people laugh. Now I know . . . I just imitate other people. I do the sort of things they do, and crack the gags they'd like to be able to tell – if they were quick enough!

'In Liverpool, everyone talks with their hands. And although they walk quite normally, nearly everyone tends to hop when they step on or off a kerb-side.

'You can never run dry of comedy material on Merseyside.' And he tells what he says is a true story:

There was a court case which went on all week in Liverpool. On the Friday, the clerk of the court suddenly noticed that there was one juror short.

He said, 'Who is acting as your foreman?'

One bloke stood up and said, 'Me, sir.'

The clerk said, 'You are one juryman short.'

'Yes', said the jury foreman, 'That's Charlie. He got fed up, so he went off to Haydock.'

And then he added, without batting an eyelid, 'But he's left his verdict with me.'

The bad days, of singing for thirty bob a week, are over for Tom O'Connor. He now lives in an expansive detached house in Formby, Lancashire, with two cars in the garage. He has security in plenty.

But it's not always been so cushy. He has 'died', he admits, a few times in the clubs, just like most other comedians, no matter how good they may think they are.

The first time was in a working men's club in Sunderland, reputed to be the toughest area in Britain to work comedy. 'I died on my feet,' recalls Tom. 'It was a Monday, but it should have been a Good Friday – because that audience crucified everybody that day.'

Once, playing a club in Wales, he trudged a mile up a hill in thick snow to put in an appearance, and only one man turned up in the audience. But the club manager insisted that Tom go on and do his act – in two separate half-hour spots.

Tom protested that it was ridiculous. He couldn't tell jokes to just one man. So the manager hastily brought three women from behind the bar and made them sit with the man, therefore boosting the size of the audience to four. 'The manager made me stay on until 11.30 pm, even though the snow was getting thicker outside. He kept saying, "A coach load of customers might arrive at any time."'

On another occasion, again in Wales, Tom found that when the audience was unfriendly, they showed it quite clearly – by turning their backs to the stage, reading their newspapers, and throwing peanuts over their shoulders at the poor comic.

That is why, perhaps, Tom O'Connor is more astute than most when he prefers to stay on as a schoolteacher, and keep his joke-telling as a part-time business. Even though it's become a very profitable hobby indeed.

A fellow bought a parrot and sent it to his granny for a birthday present. Next time he visited her, he said, 'And how's the parrot?'
She said: 'Oh it was delicious. The flesh just fell away.'

It's so slack on the docks these days, that blokes are actually taking stuff back.

The wife who was always complaining to her husband, 'You never take me anywhere.' So next day, he gave her a nudge in bed at 5.30 am, and said, 'Hey, are you coming to work with me?'

Two blokes eating their sandwiches in the factory. One of them is jumping up and down like a maniac.
The foreman says, 'What's wrong with him?'
His mate says, 'He wants to go to the toilet.'
Foreman: 'Well, why doesn't he go?'
He says, 'What – in his dinner-hour?'

Charlie is staggering home, very drunk one night. And just for a dare, with his mate, he climbs up on to the roof of the new Catholic Cathedral in Liverpool – to prove he can do it. Just then a woman comes in and kneels in prayer inside the Cathedral. She raises her head to heaven, and prays in a loud voice: 'Mother of God, please help me.'
Charlie can't resist it, so he shouts down in a booming voice, 'What do you want?'
The woman looks up and says, 'It's your mother I want, not you.'

The poor woman who sent a letter to God. 'Please Lord, I'm really desperate, I need £100 for back rent, otherwise I'm going to be evicted. Please do something to help me.' She didn't know where to send the letter, so eventually posted it to 'God, C/o the GPO.'

The letter was opened by a kindly Post Office sorter, who felt so sorry for the old dear that he quickly organised a whip-round among his mates. Between them, they managed to scrape together £96, and they sent it off to the woman by registered post. The woman opened the letter. Next day, another letter arrived at the GPO from the woman. It read: 'Dear God, thank you very much for the money. But there was four pounds short. It was probably one of those robbing swine from the Post Office.'

The lady who goes on a ship's cruise for the first time in her life. She's been aboard one night when she is invited to eat at the Captain's table, for dinner.

She says, 'What? At the prices I'm paying, eat with the crew!?'

Nurse: 'Do you want a bedpan?'
Patient (in hospital for the first time): 'Blimey, have you got to do your own cooking in here?'

The wife was getting very amorous one night with her husband, after 15 years of marriage. She turned to him and said, 'I'm going to nibble your ear, just like I used to.'
The husband said, 'By the time you find your teeth, I'll be fast asleep.'

There was this bloke who marched up a great hill, pulling a wheelbarrow full of huge logs. When he got to the top, he said to his mate, 'Hey, Harry, you've got Everton in this week's football sweep.'
Harry said, 'Who's got Nottingham Forest?'
He said, 'I think I have, in this flamin' wheelbarrow!'

The drunk on the train, who leans out of the window when the train pulls into a station, and says, 'Excuse me, porter, but where are we?'
Porter: 'Leatherhead.'
Passenger: 'And the same to you, pig-face.'

Two little boys on a bus. One boy said, 'I'm six, how old are you?'
The other said, 'I don't know.'
'Well, do women worry you?'
He said, 'No.'
The other fellow said, 'Well, you're about four.'

This fellow's wife had teeth like the Ten Commandments . . . all broken. When she was a bride, she wore a dress of white silk – Her brother was in the Paratroopers.

My brother never works. He's in the Dole Protection Society. They pay a bob a week, and if the dole people find you a job, these fellows fight your case . . .

He had to go before this Tribunal. Three of them sitting on the Bench. One said to him: 'What's your name?'
Our kid said, 'Moses.'
The second fellow said: 'Where do you come from?'
He said, 'Israel.'
The third member of the panel said, 'Well go home, and tell your wife the Three Wise Men have just stopped your dole.'

I remember when our kid proposed to his wife. He said, 'Will you marry me?'
She said, 'I'm not very good looking.'
He said, 'That's all right, you'll be out at work all day.'

You should see their house, it's one of those semi-condemned. You know, the kind of place where you wipe your feet when you come out!
Charlie bought a pig and took it home. His wife said, 'Where are you going to keep that?'
He said, 'In the house.'
She said, 'What about the smell?'
He replied, 'The pig will have to get used to it.'

This friend of mine got a job in the sewers. But he had to give it up, because he said the foreman suffered from bad breath!

It's a tough place, Liverpool. This chap turned to a fellow behind him in the bus queue and he said, 'Who are you pushing?'
He said, 'I don't know. What's your name?'

Some very famous people come from Liverpool. Noah came from Liverpool, y'know. Remember, he was just about to sail and two animals came up on the quayside, and he popped his head out and shouted, 'Are you looking for a nark?'

We haven't had a single case of Asian 'flu in Liverpool this year . . . The dockers have refused to handle it.

The Census fellow came to this fellow's house. He opened the door, and the man said, 'Is this your wife?'
Fred said, 'Of course she is. I wouldn't live in sin with an old bag like that, would I?'

Chapter Eight
JOS WHITE

Jos White is black. He's been black most of his life. And it won't rub off, he'll tell you. Just as he will readily joke about his colour all night long if you'll let him.

He was born in Liverpool. His father was an African from Sierra Leone, and his mother was from Yorkshire. His real name is Joshua Lewis. He took the name White when he turned to the stage. ('I figured that if Cilla, with a surname like White, could call herself Black, then I could call myself White.')

Jos first started out as a would-be comedian while doing his National Service in the RAF. 'We had an annual camp concert, and I went along one day, got up and told a few jokes. The lads laughed a lot and seemed to like me. I began to think there might be a future in it.' He makes it all sound so simple.

When he was demobbed he got a job as a fitter in the Merseyside shipyard of Cammell Laird, in Birkenhead, and started doing shows, as a comedian, in pubs and clubs in his spare time.

One night, he was appearing in a club, but not going down too well with the audience. 'If you don't laugh, I'll come and live next door to you – that'll bring down the price of your house.'

He said it with some venom. The audience howled. He knew then that he was on to a winner.

Ever since, Jos has deliberately built up his act to emphasise the colour problem.

'I've worked all over the country, from London and Southampton to Sunderland and Scotland, and I've never had any real trouble with audiences not appreciating my jokes,' he says proudly.

He is often saucy with some of his gags, but never what he calls naughty.

('I used to be the only docker in Liverpool who got dirt money for unloading flour.')

'My only aim is to make people laugh, in any way I can,' he says. 'I tell racial jokes because I want people to laugh, nothing more.' He insists there are no hidden messages in his brand of humour. 'No politics, no social messages.

'I've no discrimination at all – not even against Pakistanis,' he quips.

'Everyone in this country should emigrate. And the place to go to is Africa . . . it's empty!

'Let's face it,' he says candidly, 'It's true isn't it? If a coloured man comes to live next door, it does bring the price of your property down. I know that.'

He's on only nodding terms with his own neighbours, he'll tell you. Just like the rest of us.

Jos turned full-time pro four years ago, and he has been busy ever since. He appeared on *Opportunity Knocks*, and won the show, in 1968.

He writes most of his own material. 'People often tell me jokes, but I also originate a lot of my own.'

Enoch Powell doesn't want to go to Heaven when he dies – in case they make him sing Negro spirituals . . .

I know a man who is so prejudiced, that he won't even let his wife watch colour TV!

'But I will never embarrass anybody if I can avoid it,' says Jos, who has pretty strong feelings about the professional jealousy *The Comedians* has caused among the ranks of the long-established TV comics. 'Some of them should get off their backsides and try playing four spots a night in the Yorkshire clubs – and then go back two months later with the same gags. They'd die,' he says. 'Working the clubs is a hell of a lot tougher than working on TV.'

I like to make coloured people happy. You've got blonde hair, blue eyes, pink cheeks – and you say we're coloured!

Oh, wait until we take over . . . It's only a matter of time – we've got the Labour Exchanges already!

The Isle of Wight is going when we take over. And we're going to make Blackpool the capital.

It's all right you laughing, but I've got a coloured feller living next door to me, so I know what it's like. They're all over the place, aren't they?

I saw a Pakistani milkman. He had 'Co-Op' all over his turban.
I said, 'Where are you from?'
He said, 'Pakistan'.
I said, 'By gum, you've got a helluva big round, haven't you?'

This fellow living next door to me is really coloured – he's Chinese. One day a fellow knocked on his door, and said, 'Excuse me, sir, I'm from the soap company. Do you wash in Tide?'
This Chink said, 'Yes, I wash in Tide.'
The man said, 'And why do you wash in Tide?'
The Chink said, 'Well, it's too ruddy cold to wash out-tide.'

Enoch Powell was seen crying on top of a cliff. Someone said, 'Why are you crying?'
He said, 'I just saw this bus load of Pakistanis go over the edge of the cliff.'
He said, 'And you're crying about it – why?'
Enoch said, 'There were two empty seats.'

Enoch Powell died and went up to the gates of Heaven.
He rang the bell, and a big voice shouted out, 'Who dat out der?'
Enoch, said, 'Forget it!'

This Chinese knocked at my front door. I said, 'Go round the back'. Well, it's not nice is it? All the rice on the path! . . .
He said to me, 'My house same size as your house. Me decorate the rooms. How many rolls of wallpaper you buy for front parlour?'
I said, 'Sixteen rolls.'

A week later, he came back. 'I've decorated my parlour, and I've got six rolls left over.'
I said, 'So have I.'

I bought my wife a new corset last week. A one-piece corset. She slipped into it, but had a terrible job getting it on. Now she has a 22-inch waist, and a 44 inch neck!

I call my wife Treasure. Well, I took her in a pub one night, and a fellow said, 'Hell, where did you dig that up?'

When we got married, my wife looked lovely. She was all in yellow. She looked like a Christmas pudding with custard on.

The wife was moaning about me going out at night. So I took her with me to the pub one night. I said, 'What will you drink?'
She said, 'The same as you.' So I got her a pint of bitter.
She took one mouthful, and spat it out.
I said, 'What's the matter?'
She said, 'I don't know how you drink that stuff, it's horrible.'
I said, 'There you are! I told you, didn't I? – and you think I'm out enjoying myself every night!'

My lad came home from school last week, much earlier than usual.
I said, 'You've been sent home, haven't you?'
He said, 'Yes.'
I said, 'What for?'
He said, 'The lad sitting next to me was smoking.'
I said, 'Well, what did they send you home for?'
He said, 'It was me that set him on fire.'

I asked my little boy what he wanted to be when he grows up.
He said, 'A lollipop man.'
I said, 'A lollipop man? Why?'
He said, 'Cos I won't have to start work until I'm 65.'

Everyone's on strike these days, aren't they? I heard two Liverpool dockers talking the other day.
One fellow said, quite innocently, 'I see the daffodils are out.'
And the other bloke said, 'Are we going out in sympathy?'

My grandfather was actually half Indian and half Irish . . . His name was Tom O'Hawk!

My little lad came home last week and said, 'Dad, they won't let me in the swimming baths.'
So I took him round to the baths, and I said to the attendant, 'Why won't you let my boy swim in the baths?'
He said, 'Because he keeps making water in the pool.'
I laughed and said, 'Well, all the kids do that, don't they?'
The attendant said, 'Yes, but not from the high diving board!'

Chapter Nine
BERNARD MANNING

BERNARD MANNING is a big man – in every way. But particularly around the waist. If he wasn't so big, in fact, he'd probably fall off his wallet!

George Roper says of Manning: 'His mother would have been better off with a spin-drier!' But this is simply because Manning and Roper have a back-stage running 'battle' going whenever they both appear in the studios at the same time.

They joke about each other's size, and throw gags at each other which they know will 'needle' slightly. (Manning says of Roper: 'He's got more chins than a Chinese telephone directory').

Bernard also infuriates some of his fellow comedians by deliberately going on and telling the same jokes they have lined up for the show. He does this just to tease them.

Sammy Thomas once said on the TV show: 'Bernard Manning was found outside his club in Manchester, bound and gagged. The police have issued a statement to the effect that it wasn't his own gag.'

Undoubtedly, Bernard was the wealthiest of the bunch, before they all made their bow on *The Comedians*. He is the owner of a flourishing nightclub – the Embassy – in Collyhurst, Manchester, where he is resident compere, singer and comic.

(George Roper: 'Manning's club is not so much a club, more an ash-tray with music.').

The Manning family have done well out of the club business for some years. Bernard runs the Embassy, helped out by his wife Vera, and his mother, while his brother Frank runs a club in Newquay, Cornwall, and his two sisters, Alma and Rene, manage a hotel and club in Cornwall.

There were five children in the Manning family, in Ancoats, Manchester. Dad was a greengrocer, and he brought up the children as strict Roman Catholics.

Bernard left school at 14, and went to work, making cigarettes in a tobacco factory. It was there that he first started singing. 'To take my mind off the millions of flippin' cigarettes, I used to sing while I worked.'

The bosses encouraged him, presumably to help production along. It developed into a kind of Cigarette Sing-Along. But when he entered a talent contest, at the age of 17, and took home first prize – 'a pot doll' – he was in trouble with his father. 'I got a right old leathering because I shouldn't even have been in the pub, I was too young,' says Bernard, now smiling at the thought.

His singing activities were therefore curtailed, until he went into the Army for National Service, when he found himself singing with the unit dance band in the Manchester Regiment, serving in Germany.

On demob, he went into the family greengrocery business, but continued singing, part-time, in working-men's clubs around the North. His first full week's booking as a singer earned him £14 at the Oldham Empire, and shortly afterwards Bernard joined the Oscar Rabin band as resident singer, and travelled all over the country with them, as a professional.

It was only when he grew tired of working and travelling with the band that he returned to Manchester, and got a job as a compere, cracking gags in between his songs, at the Northern Sporting Club.

I'd never get married again. Had two wives, that was enough. They both died. The first one died eating poisoned mushrooms. And the second wife died of a fractured skull . . . She wouldn't eat her mushrooms!

Then he went to his father and advised him to sell the greengrocery business and put the money into a nightclub. But his father protested: 'I don't know anything about night clubs.' 'No,' said Bernard, 'But I do.'

His father relented, and they took over an old billiard saloon, and converted it into the plushy Embassy Club. The Mannings soon took over management of two other clubs.

One night, back in 1963, Bernard was appearing at the Wilton Club in Manchester, when he was told by Freddie Garrity, of Freddie and The Dreamers, that a Granada producer called Johnnie Hamp was in the audience. 'I went out on stage, threw in all my best gags, hoping to be discovered for TV,' remembers Bernard. 'I did an absolute "bomb", brought the house down with 45 minutes of songs, gags, impressions, the lot. I learned later that Hamp had left the club before I went on. I was furious.'

Because of his own club commitments, Bernard was absolutely unknown outside of Manchester before *The Comedians* hit the screen. Now, however, he is accepting other dates at clubs away from his own, and he joined the line-up of comedians playing at the London Palladium.

When he heard they were to play the London Palladium, Bernard cheekily bought a half-page advert in 'The Stage' to say: 'After 23 years of messing about, I've finally made the Grades!'

He always goes on stage smoking a large cigar. 'I get through about five a day. They're better than cigarettes. They make me cough more easily.'

With specialising in Jewish jokes, many people think Bernard is Jewish. 'I'm not,' he says, 'I'm a not-very-good Catholic. But travelling around with the Oscar Rabin band, I picked up a lot of Jewish gags.

'*One of my best mates is a Jewish salesman. I don't mean he sells Jews . . . he's not that good!*'

He also puts on shows at his club for Jewish, as well as other charities, and has raised thousands of pounds.

In *The Comedians* New Year's Eve programme, Bernard was given a song spot for the first time on TV. This resulted in him landing a recording contract, as a singer. His first LP, *The Serious Side of Bernard Manning* has now been released. 'It's ironic,' he says. 'When I was a singer, no record company wanted to know me. Then, when I turn comedian, they give me a recording contract as a singer!'

Married with one son – Bernie junior, aged 11 – Bernard drives around in a big American car (he's got to have a big car in order to get into it!), and also prefers American comedians to

British. His own favourite funny men are George Burns and Jack Benny.

He is quite uncompromising with his audiences. He throws in many a 'blue' or naughty gag. 'If they don't like me, they can always leave,' he says. 'Anyway, jokes that are a bit near the knuckle always get the biggest laughs. Women, in particular, like an occasional dirty joke – I know that for a fact.

'When it comes to telling jokes,' he boasts, 'I can hold my own with anybody. I recently took on a bet that I could go on stage and tell jokes, non-stop, for an hour. I won the bet, and was still going strong for nearly 90 minutes. Nobody can follow me when I play a club in Manchester. But nobody.'

Big words. But, as I say, he's a big man in every way, our Bernard.

Two Irishmen in prison.
Paddy: 'How long are you in for?'
Mick: 'Twenty seven years. How long are you in for?'
Paddy: 'Twenty five years.'
Mick: 'Well, you'd better sleep near the door, because you get out before me.'

George Best has been down to London to get a little peace and quiet ... He's found the piece, now he's hoping she'll keep quiet!

I know a fellow who won a trip to China ... He's still out there, trying to win a trip back!

Mrs. Mills has joined Women's Lib. She burned her bra in Trafalgar Square yesterday, and it took four fire brigades to put it out.

A fellow went to the local council and complained: 'It's about the roof on my house.'
Councillor: 'What about it?'
Man: 'We'd like one.'

Charlie: 'We've got bugs in the bedroom.'
Councillor: 'Well, pull the bed away from the wall.'
Charlie: 'We did . . . but they pull it back again. I threw a bucket of petrol on them the other night, and the bugs came out on motor-bikes!'

'These houses are hopeless. The walls are so thin, I opened the oven door the other day to look at the Sunday joint, and the fellow from next door was dipping his bread in our gravy.'

An Irishman walks into a pub with a big door under his arm. The barman says, 'What's the idea of the door, Paddy?'
Irishman says, 'Well, last night, I lost my key.'
Barman: 'Well, what happens if you lose the door?'
Paddy says, 'It's all right . . . I've left the window open.'

'I'm the only fellow who works around here. The fellow next door to me is so lazy. The last job he had was school prefect . . . One of his insurance stamps is worth more than a Penny Black.'

Two lunatics out fishing. It was like the Sea of Galilee all over again, the boat was full of fish. One fellow said, 'I hope you marked the water where the fishing was so good.'
The other fellow said, 'Oh yes, I put a chalk mark on the side of the boat.'
The first fellow said, 'You stupid ass – we might not get that boat next time out.'

Bernard Delfont is passing a building site. He sees this fellow do three double somersaults, a jack-knife, a back flip, and land on his feet. Delfont says, 'I'll book you for the London Palladium.'
The foreman says, 'You'd better book big Paddy with him.'
Delfont says, 'Why?'
The foreman says, 'Because he's the fellow that hit him on the hand with the sledgehammer.'

The bailiff came to serve the summons. The occupier of the house next door to me was hiding behind the door with a pair of bellows.
Every time the bailiff put the summons under the door, this fellow blew it back out again. The bailiff went back to the Town Hall, and said, 'I didn't get the rent. And I wouldn't pay any rent for a draughty house like that, either.'

A notice seen recently in a Jewish tailor's shop-window in Belfast: 'Buy now while shops last.'

A fellow woke up after an operation. The doctor said, 'We've managed to save one of your eyes.'
He said, 'Thanks very much.'
The doctor said, 'Yes, we'll give it to you on your way out.'

A fellow walked into the barber's shop and said, 'Give me a Tony Curtis hair cut.' The barber shaved every hair off his head. He was as bald as a billiard ball. The fellow was livid.
He said, 'You great berk, do you know who Tony Curtis is?'
The barber said, 'Of course I do – I saw him in "The King and I" fourteen times.'

Hymie Goldberg said to his wife: 'My darling Rosie, what would you like for your birthday? A nice mink coat?'
She said, 'No, I'm 67, I've got a mink coat. What would I do with another one? Why don't you buy me a nice, shaded plot in the Garden of Rest – for the future?'
So he did. He bought her the best plot in the Jewish cemetery. The following year, she said to him, 'Hymie, what are you going to buy me for my birthday? I'm 68 tomorrow.'
He said, 'Nothing – you never used last year's present.'

A fellow in the zoo, standing there, pulling tongues at the snakes.
The zoo-keeper came up and said, 'What are you doing that for?'
He said, 'Well, they started it!'

An Irish woman in court. She said, 'I want a divorce from that man Paddy O'Ryan.'
The Judge said, 'Has he been cruel to you? Or left you short of money?'
She said, 'No, he's always been reasonably generous.'
Judge: 'Well has he ever beaten you?'
She said, 'No, he's never laid a finger on me in my whole life.'
Judge: 'Well, has he ever been unfaithful?'
She said, 'Ah yes, we've got him there. My last four kids weren't his.'

An Irishman telephoned Dublin. When a voice answered, he said, 'Is that Dublin double-two double-two?'

The voice said, 'No, this is Dublin 2222.'
The first fellow said, 'Oh, I'm sorry to have bothered you.'
Back came the reply: 'That's all right, sir. The phone was ringing anyway.'

This little Jewish fellow got knocked down in an accident. He was rushed to hospital. The nurse tucked him into bed, propped up the pillows. 'Mr. Cohen, are you comfortable?'
He said, 'Well, I've got four shops! I'm not complaining.'

A woman went to the doctors. He said to her, 'Mrs. Jones, I've got some good news for you.'
She said, 'I'm not married.'
Doctor: 'Well, Miss Jones, I've got some bad news for you . . .'

Mr. Kosygin is going round a big British factory with Mr. Ted Heath.
Kosygin: 'What time do they start work here?'
Mr. Heath: 'About eight o'clock.'
Kosygin: 'In my country, the workers start at six o'clock. Any breaks?'
Heath: 'Oh yes, they knock off at ten o'clock for a cup of tea and a bun.'
Kosygin: 'In Russia, we have no breaks. How long for dinner?'
Heath: 'About an hour. But some of them like a bet, so they might take a bit longer.'
Kosygin: 'In Russia, they have ten minutes for dinner. Sandwiches, they buy from a machine. What time do they finish work?'
Heath: 'Oh, they're off just after four o'clock. All off home in their cars to watch *Children's Hour* on telly.'
Kosygin: 'In Russia, they work till ten o'clock at night. From six o'clock until 10 pm.'
Heath: 'Oh, you couldn't get these lads in Britain to work like that.'
Kosygin: 'Why not?'
Heath: 'Because they're all flamin' Communists.'

Two Jews about to be shot by the Gestapo. The order is given: 'Ready, take aim . . .''
Hymie steps forward, daringly, and shouts: 'You dirty, lousy Germans – knickers to Adolf Hitler!'
His mate Abie says: 'Look Hymie – don't start causing trouble!'

A girl went to see her friend who had just recently been married, and she said to her: 'I thought you didn't like Catholics?'

The newly-wed said, 'I don't.'

She said, 'Well, why have you got a picture of the Pope over the mantelpiece?'

She said, 'Is that the Pope?'

The other one said, 'Yes.'

The bride said, 'My husband told me it was Francis Lee in his international cap.'

An Irishman went to a car scrapyard, and said, 'Have you got a door for a 15 cwt. truck?'

The dealer said, 'Yes, we have sir. Five pounds.'

He said, 'Five pounds? They only cost fifty bob down the road.'

Dealer: 'Well, why don't you go and buy one down the road, then?'

Irishman: 'Because they haven't got any left. They've sold out.'

Dealer: Well, when we've got none in, ours are only fifty bob.'

The Irishman says, 'Thank you very much, sir. I'll come back when you've got none.'

A fellow goes into a tobacconists.

'A packet of cigarettes, please!'

Shopkeeper: 'Ten or Twenty?'

'Twenty.'

Shopkeeper: 'Turkish, or Virginia?'

'Virginia.'

Shopkeeper: 'Cork tipped or plain?'

'Cork tipped.'

Shopkeeper: 'Do you want a soft pack or a hard pack?'

He said, 'Never mind, I've packed up smoking.'

There's this blind fellow sitting in the golf clubhouse at St. Andrews, and Arnold Palmer walks in. This fellow says, 'Is that Mr. Arnold Palmer, the great American golfer?'

Palmer says, 'It is friend. Nice to meet you.'

He says, 'It's always been my ambition, Mr. Palmer, to play you at golf.'

Palmer says, 'Friend, it's my privilege. We'll have a game, and just to make it interesting, shall we have a little side bet for a dollar a hole?'

This fellow says, 'I thought we'd play for three hundred quid a hole.'

Palmer, a bit put out by this, says, 'OK, if that's the way you want it, that suits me fine. What time do you want to play?'
The blind fellow says, 'At midnight, tonight.'

Little Harry Cohen is in hospital. It says on his card 'An enema.' The nurse came and gave him one, but forgot to mark his card. Five minutes later, another nurse gave him an enema. She forgot to mark it on the card, and six different nurses came and gave him the same thing. He went missing, and they had a search for him. He was found hiding in the toilet. They knocked on the door. 'Is that you, Mr. Cohen?'
His weak voice came through the door: 'Is that a friend – or an enema?'

Hymie Goldberg died, and they were reading his will. 'To my lovely wife Miriam, I leave one million pounds cash. To my dear son Benjamin, whom I love and cherish, I leave one million pounds cash. To Rosie, my daughter, I leave the store, a Rolls Royce Silver Cloud, and half-a-million in cash. And to my brother-in-law Louis, who always said I would never remember him in my will, and never did a day's work in his life . . . Hello Louis!'

An Irishman, a Scotsman and a Jew were all condemned to death in America. So it's the gas chamber. Before they went in, they were each asked, 'Any last requests?'
The Scotsman said, 'Yes, I'd like a bottle of whisky. Bell's please.'
The Irishman said, 'I'll take a crate of Guinness in with me.'
The Jew said, 'I'd like to take a piano in with me.'
Three hours later, they opened the door, and the Irishman and the Scotsman are both stone cold dead. But the little Jew is still sitting there, playing the piano.
The Doctor said, 'I can't understand this – how have you managed to survive that gas?'
And the little Jew said, 'Tunes help you breathe more easily!'

Chapter Ten
GEORGE ROPER

THERE WAS THIS *man standing at the bus-stop. He was wearing wellies and eating a meat pie. Behind him in the queue stood a woman, with a poodle on a lead. The poodle kept jumping up, trying to get a bite of the fellow's meat pie, so he turned to the lady and said: 'Missus, can I throw your dog a bit?'*

The woman smiled gratefully and said, 'Yes.'

So he picked up the dog and threw it fifty yards down the road!

Funny? It's a howler. And this was the joke which launched the podgy Liverpudlian George Roper on an unsuspecting TV public. The first joke that really made an impact for him on *The Comedians*, and prompted producer John Hamp to sign George up on a long-term contract.

George likes jokes about wellies. In fact he specialises in them. Everyone wears wellies in George's mind. 'Even the Queen wears wellies when it's raining, doesn't she?' he says simply. 'And some people wear wellies when it isn't.'

Wellies – even the mere mention of the word – make people laugh. And George now finds that he can introduce a pair of wellies into any joke he tells.

His fascination for wellies (Wellington boots, for the un-initiated!) goes back to his employment some years ago as a labourer with Wimpey's (the builders, not the hot-dog merchants!). 'Everyone used to wear wellies. Me included. It was standard footwear,' he recalls.

And he's now become so popular with his welly jokes that, when he was in the TV studio recording one programme, George was hit flush on the nose with a pair of tiny rubber boots. They were thrown by an over-enthusiastic woman sitting in the audience.

('I've had some things thrown at me in my time, but never before a pair of wellies').

They were little red wellies, bearing the note: 'The best of luck – I like your welly jokes. Mary.' George took them home, and tried them on his two children – Nicholas and Louise. The trouble was, they didn't fit either of them.

George has been a pro comedian since 1965. His real ambition at one time was to be a pilot. But the RAF couldn't agree to this . . . for a start, they couldn't find a plane big enough!

He was born in Norris Green, Liverpool, now lives in Manchester, and is one of the most popular characters on the Northern nightclub circuit.

He's another comic who has known poverty. There were five children in the Roper family, three girls and two boys. Dad saw a lot of life – he was a window cleaner.

'Times were hard when I started at school, in the early war years,' says George. 'We never went without, but a jam-butty was often a meal.'

On leaving school, he went straight into the Merchant Navy, following his brother Bernard. He worked as a galley-boy for Moss Hutchinson Line, and then went on the New York run, working in the kitchens and later becoming a steward.

But George was unlucky with his ships. One – the *Empress of Canada* – went on fire, and another – the *Franconia* – broke down at sea. (The breakdown had nothing to do with the ship being overloaded, despite the ever-increasing weight of a certain steward!)

Redundant from the Navy, he joined the RAF, and instead of becoming a pilot he became a drill instructor. It was while he was in the RAF, and stationed in Holland, that George started entertaining with a Forces concert party.

He met old-timer Sandy Powell, who encouraged him enormously and told him to forget about the theatre, which was dying, and concentrate instead on TV and night-clubs.

When he left the RAF, after six years, he worked as an electrician's mate ('I was always a live wire, anyway'), and started entertaining in pubs at week-ends for extra cash. This meant singing *Won't You Come Home, Bill Bailey* and other such gay, scintillating songs, for thirty-five shillings a week.

George did a stint at a holiday camp in Morecambe, in 1964, working in the kitchens during the day, and on stage as an entertainer in the evenings. His decision to turn pro came the day he was offered one night's booking for £5 at Widnes.

For £5 a night, he'd sing and tell jokes until the cows came home! He had never earned anything like £25 a week before. But he had done no TV at all, until a phone call came from Johnnie Hamp offering him a spot on the first programme of *The Comedians*.

'I was not at all impressed with the first run-through,' says George. 'I certainly never dreamed it would build up into a long-running series, and make us all instantly recognised "faces." '

His first marriage ended in divorce. He met his second wife, Linda, working in a dry cleaners, where he used to regularly take his suits. She suited him down to the ground. So he took off his wellies, and married her. She was generous to him, in that she only charged him the normal price for each suit, despite the fact that George's suits were as big as bell tents.

Someone else who discovered this was the thief who broke into George's car, one night, and stole his favourite mohair suit, an expensive one he had especially made for *The Comedians*.

George appeared on TV to appeal for the return of the suit, but he never saw it again. 'Whoever nicked it would be in for a shock when he tried it on,' he said. 'It fitted me perfectly, but the thief would probably be able to get his wife and family into it as well.'

There is always the possibility, of course, that the thief had the suit taken apart – and six new ones made-to-measure from the material.

Weight is a problem with George. ('It's brought on through silly things, like eating and drinking, you know!') He now touches the scales at around 18 stone. But he enjoys being fat. He thinks that his seven chins help viewers to laugh at him, as well as his jokes!

('George Roper?' laughs Bernard Manning. 'He's about as funny as a bout of typhoid fever!').

A fellow in his wellies rushed into the doctor's surgery, and said, 'Quick doctor, can you deal with an emergency?'
The Doctor said, 'No, not today.'
He said, 'Please yourself! Only your waiting room is on fire!'

Two Irishmen in court. Magistrate (to Paddy): 'Where do you live?'
Paddy: 'I've no fixed abode.'
Magistrate (to Mick): 'And where do you live?'
Mick: 'In the flat above him.'

A little lad in school. They've been learning the alphabet.
Teacher says: 'Now Tommy, what comes after T?'
He said, 'The six o'clock news, Miss.'

Two little boys are playing with their toys at Christmas.
One says, 'Hey, Charlie, I wanted a budgie for Christmas, but I'm not worried. This tortoise I've got can fly just as good as a budgie.'
Charlie: 'Tortoises can't fly.'
He said, 'They can if you throw them hard enough.'

A fellow went to the doctors, and said: 'I can't stop smoking.'
The doctor said, 'Try wine gums.'
He came a fortnight later. 'They're no good.'
Doctor: 'Why not?'
The fellow said, 'I have trouble lighting 'em.'

A fellow dashes into a pub and says, 'Quick, give me a pint of bitter, before the row starts.'
The landlord gives him a pint, and he knocks it back in one gulp.
'Give me another pint, before the row starts.'
So he gives him another, and he finishes that.
'Another pint please, before the row starts.'
The landlord says, 'Hey, what's all this about a row starting?'
The fellow said, 'Well, I've got no money.'

An Irishman went to a plastic surgeon, and said, 'Are you the famous Harley Street plastic surgeon?'
He said, 'I am, yes, I am.'
The Irishman said, 'Is there any chance of you putting a new handle on our polythene bucket?'

What do you call an Irishman who says he's got ten O Levels?
– A liar!

An Irishman threw a petrol bomb across the room in Yates's Wine Lodge, Manchester, last week. One of the customers picked it up, and drank it!

An Irishman went to the building site. The Foreman said, 'Are you looking for a job?'
He said, 'I am, yis, I am.'
The Foreman said, 'Can you work with a wheelbarrow?'
Irishman: 'Oh, I don't know nothing about machinery.'

An Irishman wearing wellies got knocked down by a bus. It knocked his left ear off. He went running down the street after the bus. A policeman said, 'What are you looking for?'
He said, 'I'm looking for my left ear.'
The copper said, 'Well, it's no good to you now.'
Irishman: 'No, but my cigarette was behind it.'

I'm very keen on football, y'know. I went to Manchester United last week, walked through the turnstiles at Old Trafford and gave the bloke on the gate a fiver and said, 'Two please.'
He said, 'Do you want two full backs or two half backs?'

I phoned up Sir Matt Busby and said, 'What time is the kick-off on Saturday?'
He said, 'What time can you get here?'

Dennis Law scored a good goal the other day. Did you see it . . . on *All Our Yesterdays*?

I went to this dance in Blackpool. It was a funny place – all fellers! I said, 'Where are all the birds?' This feller said, 'It's a man's club, and we dance with each other.'
I said, 'Well, who are those two big strapping fellows on the bandstand, in their wellies? Are they the chuckers-out?'
He said, 'No, they're the spot prizes!'

A fellow came running down the dock road, and he was stopped by a policeman. The copper said, 'Why are you running?'
He said, 'I'm having a race with this bloke for a pint of bitter.'
So the policeman let him go.

Another fellow dashed up, puffing and panting, and said to the policeman, 'Why did you let him go?'

The policeman said, 'He's only having a race for a pint of bitter.'

The man said, 'I know, but I'm the landlord – and he hasn't paid for it!'

A Liverpool docker was walking along the dock road, in his wellies, beating a tortoise to death. A policeman said, 'What did you do that for?'

The docker said, 'It was getting on my nerves. It's been following me about all day.'

Three fellows up on a mountain. One said, 'Why do you do it, old chap? Why do you go mountaineering?'

The second fellow said, 'I do it for the sheer enjoyment of it, old boy. How about you?'

The first fellow said, 'The very same reason. It's so exhilarating, so refreshing, such a marvellous challenge.'

They turned to the third fellow, an Irishman, standing there in his wellies.

'What about you? Why do you climb mountains?'

The Irishman said, 'Climb it? I'm here to move it!'

A fellow in a helicopter was flying over Liverpool docks, taking photographs. But one of the pictures didn't turn out . . . one of the dockers moved!

A bloke went to the doctor's, and said, 'I feel like a steering wheel.'

Doctor: 'How do you mean?'

He said, 'I get these awful turns.'

An Irishman goes for his first driving lesson. He says to the driving instructor: 'Will it be OK if I drive around in my wellies?'

The instructor said, 'Let's try it with the car first.'

Hear about the fellow in Manchester who got charged in court with using a four-letter word in Old Trafford football ground? He shouted 'Goal!'

Heard the one about the Jewish jockey, who kept winning his races by a nose?

88

Fellow went to the doctor and said, 'I've got a terrible pain down here, doctor.'
Doctor: 'Do you have any trouble passing water?'
He said, 'No, but I sometimes feel a bit giddy when I go across a bridge.'

Two Irishmen on a plane for the first time in their lives. One said, 'Wouldn't it be awful if we fell out?'
The other said, 'Don't be silly, Paddy, we've been friends for such a long time.'

An Irishman got a job on the dustcarts. A big seven-footer, he was, wearing his wellies. He could carry four bins at once. One in each hand, one balanced on his head, and another on his right shoulder.
He used to go about whistling all the time, as he did the job.
The foreman said, 'I think it's marvellous, Irish, how do you do it?'
Irish said, 'It's easy. I just put my lips together, and blow!'

A fellow went to the insurance company and said, 'I want to insure my car against theft.'
They told him, 'You can't just insure it against theft. You've got to insure it against fire and theft.'
He said, 'Who the hell's going to pinch a burning car?'

A dustman went to a house and knocked on the door. A Pakistani opened it. 'What do you want?'
The dustman said, 'I've come about the bin.'
The Pakistani said, 'I'm very sorry – I let it yesterday!'

A man died, and his wife had him cremated and his ashes put on the mantelpiece. They had a party, and one fellow was smoking a big Havana cigar, and he kept flicking his ash into the silver-box on the mantelpiece.
A bit later, one of the dead man's relatives comes up, mournfully, took one look at the box, and said, 'What a pity he had to die so young.'
She tried to console the poor widow. She looked in the box and said, 'Yes, well he's gone now . . . but he's put on weight!'

Harry Evans went home with two black eyes, a broken arm, and he was in a shocking state.

His wife said, 'What happened?'

He said, 'Paddy gave me a good hiding.'

She said, 'Why? He's your best mate.'

Harry said, 'I said something about the Pope.'

Wife: 'Well, you shouldn't have said anything about the Pope. You know Paddy is a Catholic.'

Harry said, 'Oh yes, I knew Paddy was a Catholic – but I didn't know the Pope was.'

Bernard Manning's wife is even bigger than he is. She doesn't have a bath . . . she just goes through the car-wash!

Chapter Eleven
MIKE BURTON

MIKE BURTON – he's the fellow with the sawn-off head – could be called the oldest skinhead in the business. His short crew-cut hair style, coupled with those distinctive black-framed spectacles, now make him instantly recognised wherever he goes.

The hair style was something of an accident, really. 'It was some years ago. I was with some mates, and we all dared each other to have a close-cropped hair cut. This was long before the days of the Skinheads,' says Mike.

'When I came out of the barber's shop, I couldn't believe what he'd done to me.' He now chuckles at the experience. 'I looked like a shot goosegog. There was no option but to go to another barber immediately and ask him if he could do anything with it.' He managed to patch up Mike's hair so that it didn't look too bad, and Mike has been going to that same hairdresser in Birkenhead ever since. He doesn't need to ask for a short-back-and-sides any more!

The glasses, he has worn since he was a child. His eyesight was affected, he thinks, by an early attack of measles as an infant.

Mike is now known not just for his appearance, but also

among fellow comedians as 'The Smart Fellow.' For he's got a very way-out sense of humour, and most of his jokes are Burton tailor-made and have a degree of subtlety perhaps lacking in those of other comics.

A wealthy American businessman who is terrified of a nuclear attack. So he spends a fortune having this private anti-nuclear shelter built for his family in the middle of the Arizona Desert. It's five miles under the ground, is equipped with everything under the sun, takes three years to build and costs him eight million dollars. Finally, it's finished, and he sets off to inspect it. He gets out of his Cadillac and is just walking across the desert to the shelter entrance . . . and an Indian shoots him in the back with an arrow!

Mike comes from a docking family in Birkenhead. At 15 he left school, and worked as an order-boy for the Co-op. Two years National Service saw him as a pay clerk in the Army, based at Devizes and then Kidderminster.

When he came out of the Army, he went onto the docks, even though his father, a lifelong docker, tried to discourage him.

'The job on the docks didn't last long,' says Mike. 'I fell down a ship's hatch onto a pile of wire mesh and had a very nasty accident.' He quit the docks, and went through a series of jobs in quick succession, working as a navvy on the roads, then as a breeze-block maker (he soon caught the draught from that job!), and finally settled down as a floor-layer. ('No, I didn't lie on the floor . . . I laid floor tiles.')

The first time he ever got up to entertain in public is still only a vague memory. 'I was stoned out of my mind at the time,' says Mike. 'My mates dared me to get up and give a song. We were having a few bevvies in the Craftsman's Club, Birkenhead. I sang *Won't You Come Home, Bill Bailey* . . . I think.' Then had trouble in finding his own way home.

His first real bookings as an entertainer were for two dinners, telling a few jokes, and he got 22 shillings for the night. Even then, the agent insisted on taking his two-bob commission.

'I was awful when I first started out as a comedian,' says Mike. 'I had four jokes which I thought were marvellous. I've forgotten them now – thank goodness. Actually, I think they all died!'

Heard the one about the coal miner who couldn't stand heights? They could never get him to the surface!

Slowly, he built up a comedy act and was soon entertaining in clubs on Saturday and Sunday nights, and doing his tiling job five days a week. Then, in 1963, he gave up the job and turned full-time comic . . . and promptly found himself out of work for frequent spells.

'Times were hard,' says Mike. 'In between odd bookings, I couldn't get a decent job. I picked up about fifty bob a week on the dole. I didn't have enough money to buy a packet of fags. I even used to do baby-sitting, or wash the babies' nappies for my sister and her friends, to earn a few bob for a smoke.'

Freddie ('Parrot-Face') Davies then gave Mike a push in the right direction. He was then entertainments manager at a Butlin's holiday camp, and he gave Mike a job as a redcoat. 'I was so embarrassed,' recalls Mike. 'I hated putting on that red jacket and white flannels. I looked a right weedy sight. I think my face matched my coat most of the time.'

In 1964, he met Valerie, the woman who was to become his wife. She was head girl in a dancing troupe at the Golden Sands, Jersey.

People think my wife is Norwegian. She looks like an 'orse.

My wife is so ugly . . . Well, she went to see a horror film – and the audience thought she was making a Personal Appearance!

Over the last half-dozen years, Mike has been climbing steadily to success. He did spots in the TV shows *The Good Old Days*, *Comedy Bandbox*, *Let's Laugh* and *The Des O'Connor Show*, toured with The Bachelors, and did a season with Gerry and The Pacemakers.

'I used to specialise in "mad" gags,' says Mike. 'Really way-out gags . . .'

A fellow knocked on the door of a house. 'Is Mr. Simpson in?'
The man who opened the door said, 'I'm afraid Mr. Simpson passed away this morning.'
He said, 'Oh, I am sorry. But did he say anything about a tin of brown paint before he went?'

'But I found that people wouldn't laugh at these kind of jokes because they weren't on the same wavelength as me,' says Mike. 'So I've now changed my style, and tell more down-to-earth stories.'

Heard about the latest birth control method? It's not a pill, it's a little man. You hang this little man up on the bedpost and every five minutes he shouts: 'Don't do that!'

One of his strangest experiences was when he played a nightclub in Yorkshire, and there was no applause at all when he concluded his act. But everyone in the audience put their hands up in the air. The manager later enthusiastically said to Mike, 'You went down very well. I want to book you again.' Mike looked puzzled. 'But they didn't clap at all,' he stammered, still a little shaken at the reaction. 'Oh, they never do,' said the club manager. 'But when they like an act here, they just put their hands in the air to signal the fact.'

Heard about the Irishman who died in China?
They buried him in a paddy field.

He's always considered himself unlucky, however. On his first TV appearance, on the BBC's *The Good Old Days*, he had a six-minute spot. When the show was transmitted, Mike's contribution was edited down to just two minutes.

Then he tried looking for new scriptwriters. 'I paid one guy £25 for four new gags – and not one of them was useable. My wife read them, looked disgusted, and threw them in the bin.'

On the brighter side, a happy event came when Valerie had a baby, after several years when they thought it was impossible. Their daughter, Heidi, is now two.

With the success of *The Comedians*, Mike's fortunes have taken a turn for the better. He lives in the pleasant surroundings of Chester, plays golf – off a handicap of ten – and one of the greatest thrills of his career came in 1971 when he was presented to the Queen after appearing in the Liverpool Royal Show.

'You can become quite hardened to audiences, after working nightclubs for a long time,' says Mike. 'But at least I know now I can make the Queen laugh, because I saw her. I was dead chuffed when I caught her laughing at some of my jokes.'

A surgeon took his suit back to the tailor, and complained: 'It's all wrong.'
The tailor said, 'What's the matter with it?'
The surgeon said, 'I don't know. It was all right until I took the stitches out!'

I know a fellow who went to the local swimming baths and poured buckets of water into the deep end of the pool.

The attendant came along, and said, 'What's going on?'

This chap said, 'The diving board is too high.'

Remember those old slave ships, where they used to have slaves to row those whopping great boats? Well, the slave master came to the gang of slaves one day and said, 'I've got some good news and some bad news for you. I'll tell you the bad news first. The Captain wants some more effort from you – he wants another ten strokes an hour.'

'And the good news?' they all asked.

'Oh yes, you're all working Sunday!'

There was an Irishman in Liverpool who went to see the Olympic Committee, and said, 'I want to swim for Ireland.'

So they threw him in the River Mersey and said, 'Go ahead – it's that way!'

A fellow sitting in the stalls of the cinema, moaning and groaning. A woman went to complain to the manager about him. The manager came round, and said to him, 'What's your name?'

The bloke groaned and murmured, 'Charlie Brown.'

Manager: 'Where do you come from?'

He said, 'The balcony.'

An old man of 91 went to the Doctor for a check up. The doctor said, 'Can you come back tomorrow?'

He said, 'No, I'm going out with my Dad tomorrow.'

Doctor: 'How old is your Dad?'

He said, 'A hundred and twenty four.'

Doctor: 'Well, can you come back on Friday?'

He said, 'No, my grandfather is getting married on Friday and I've got to go to his wedding.'

Doctor: 'How old is your grandfather?'

He said, 'One hundred and fifty-eight.'

Doctor: 'What does he want to get married for?'

He said, 'Oh, he doesn't want to. He's got to!'

A coloured fellow saw this Road Safety warning on TV – 'Wear something light at night, so you can be seen by motorists!'

So he went and bought himself a white mackintosh, a white shirt, white tie, white shoes and socks, and a white hat. He went out for a walk, with his white dog . . . and got run over by a snow plough!

A fellow went to see the doctor. The doctor said, 'You need glasses.'
He said, 'How do you know?'
Doctor: 'I could tell, as soon as you walked through that window.'

I was in the pub the other day when a little weedy chap walked in and shouted angrily, 'Who the hell painted my car bright pink, outside?'
This great big feller of seven-feet-five stood up and said, 'I did.'
The little bloke said, 'Oh, well . . . I just thought I'd tell you – the first coat is dry.'

They're football mad in Manchester. Absolutely fanatical. This Manchester United supporter would get up every morning, before breakfast, put on his red and white scarf, and start whirring his rattle, shouting, 'Come on, United!' Every morning he did this, for three years.
One day he came downstairs, and his wife said, 'Do you know, Charlie, sometimes I think you love Manchester United more than you love me.'
He took one look at her, and he said, 'Listen, I love Manchester City more than I love you.'

A little Jewish fellow opened a fish-and-chip shop next door to a bank. One night, a friend went in and said, 'Hymie, can you lend me a fiver? I'm absolutely skint.'
The Jewish fellow said, 'On my life, I can't. I'm afraid I've got an agreement with the bank manager.'
He said, 'What kind of an agreement is that?'
Hymie said, 'They won't sell fish and chips, if I don't lend money.'

The father who went along to a Parents' Evening at the local school.
He said to the headmaster, 'I've come to see how my little boy is making out.'
The headmaster said, 'He's in a class of his own.'
The father said, 'Really? Oh, I didn't know he was that clever!'
The headmaster said, 'He isn't . . . but he smells!'

96

Two lunatics on a train. One said, 'I wish we were going the other way.'
His pal said, 'Why?'
He said, 'Because I like to sit with my back to the engine.'

A docker was walking out of the gates at Liverpool with a great big pumpkin under his arm. The policeman stopped him and said, 'Where do you think you're going with that?'
The docker said, 'Oh hell! Is it twelve o'clock already?'

A bloke went on holiday to the Holy Land, and he was visiting the Sea of Galilee. He said to the local fisherman with a boat, 'Can you take me across the lake?'
The fisherman said, 'Yes, certainly, sir. Five pounds a trip.'
The holidaymaker said, 'Five pounds? That's a bit steep.'
Fisherman: 'Well, remember, our Lord walked across there.'
This fellow said, 'At those prices, I'm not surprised.'

A fellow was walking through the wood one day when he saw a frog. So he said, 'Good morning, little frog.'
The frog said, 'I'm not a frog, I'm a handsome prince. This nasty old witch put a curse on me . . . but if you take me home, put me under your pillow, and sleep on me, tomorrow I'll turn into a prince again.'
So this chap did. He took the frog home, and next morning he woke up, and lying next to him was this handsome young prince.
And that, your worships, is the case for the defence!

Chapter Twelve
MIKE REID

MIKE REID is a tough character. And big with it. The sort of fellow you wouldn't like to meet on a dark night ... unless he's with you. He is the first Cockney to be signed up, long term, for *The Comedians*.

He earned his place on the show when he phoned up Johnnie Hamp in Manchester and asked for an audition. Johnnie said, 'I haven't got time for an audition – do something over the phone.'

'Over the phone?' queried Mike.

'Yes, tell me a joke,' said Johnnie.

So Mike did, though rather reluctantly. He reeled off the first gag he could remember.

(Seen in the paper today, an advert: Woman, deaf in left ear, wearing hearing-aid, would like to meet man, deaf in right ear, wearing hearing-aid. Object – stereo!)

'That's not bad,' said Johnnie. 'Let's have another.'

(Two geese flying high over the M1 when a Jumbo Jet comes screeching overhead at a helluva speed. One goose says to the other: 'Harry, I wish I could fly like that.' The other one says, 'You would, mate, if your bum was on fire.')

'You're booked,' said Johnnie. 'Come up to Manchester and

do a taping.'

It was Mike's first time in front of the TV cameras, as a comic. And from that one appearance, Reid has rocketed to stardom with his fiery, bash-bash, heavyweight brand of humour.

He was born in Hackney and went straight from school into a job as a coalman. ('I was always a big feller, and I could hump around 2 cwt. sacks even at the age of 15').

But the coal job didn't last and he did a variety of jobs in order to take home a few pounds a week. He was a steward in the Merchant Navy – New Zealand and Australia run – a brick-layer's labourer, a navvy, digging roads. 'You name it, I've done it . . . Anything to stay working. I was never out of work, never short of a bob or two.'

Briefly, he had his own business as a coal dealer. ('I bought this lorry and went out with another geezer to deliver a lorry full of coal. It was pouring with rain, and we both got soaked to the skin. Then all the coal sacks fell off the lorry. So I just threw myself flat in the gutter and lay there. This other feller throws himself down beside me, and we both had a jolly good laugh, with rainwater dripping off us').

That was it. He packed in the coal lark, and took to collecting scrap metal. 'But the gear box went on my lorry, so I parked it round the corner from home and left it. After a couple of months, someone nicked it, so I didn't even have to bovver trying to sell it.'

His entry into show business ('What a laugh that is!') came when the compere didn't turn up to do his stint at a public-house in North London, so Mike got up and sang a couple of songs – and was asked if he wanted a regular week-end job at 25 shillings a night. He jumped at it.

He started out as a singer, then did a tape-recording act, miming to musical and comedy tapes.

Ten years ago, he turned full-time professional with his singing and 'pantomime' act, and toured the American Service bases in Germany, Turkey and North Africa.

For five years, he worked as a stuntman, doing films and TV work (appearing in things like *The Saint*, *The Barron*, *The Avengers*, and a string of British feature films). He specialised in car-driving, doing daredevil stunts, because he was always fanatical about cars, even long before he was old enough to have his first driving licence.

From stuntman, he turned to comedy, and in 1971 he came

second in the Butlin's national talent contest, finishing up with a prize of £750 at the London Palladium. Mike was still disappointed, he admits. He felt he should have won it. Particularly when another comic – Joey Kaye – walked off with first prize.

'There are three things you can do with an audience. You can woo them, you can ignore them, or you can dominate them,' says Mike. 'Being a big feller, I have to be strong. I have to dominate. So I go out there and shout at them. That's my style. I hit them as hard as I can with one gag after another. And they either respond, or they don't.'

Over the last few years, he's become one of the top club comics in London, and is constantly in demand for stag nights.

Now here is a lovely, dark-skinned lady. She's come all the way from Mombasa to dance for you. And if anyone wants to take her home afterwards, they're welcome . . . 'Cos it's a long way to go!

He specialises now in skinhead gags . . .

A skinhead goes into a restaurant. 'Here, waiter, there's a worm in this meat pie.'
The waiter says, 'I beg your pardon, sir, but that's fat.'
The skinhead says, 'Yeah, well it's entitled to be, it's eaten all the meat, hasn't it?'

He admits, too, that there is a fair bit of Mike Reid in some of those skinhead routines. 'I was always a bit of a Jack the Lad. A bit lairy. A bit flash. I've cooled down a lot now, of course.'

Mike tells all kinds of stories, putting on different accents – American, Jewish, Australian, Irish, Cockney. 'I try to involve all nationalities in my act. It's essential to involve the whole audience. After all, nobody lives anywhere else, do they? They all live over here. And I've got to make them feel as though I'm not just having a go at any individual section.'

He's played the Northern club circuits a few years back, but now finds he can get all the work he wants in and around London. Essentially, he's a true Cockney.

Really, he is still out to prove himself an all-round entertainer. He still sings (mostly Frank Sinatra numbers and standards), is thoroughly at home as a compere, and also used to blow a good trumpet ('Until my lip went').

Mike is married, and has two sons – Michael, 8 and Mark, 6 –

and two stepchildren – Jimmy, 19, and Angela, 13. 'But I don't believe in telling jokes about the wife,' he chuckles.

My wife is so ugly, even as a kid they used to put her in the middle of a field to act as a scarecrow. The birds were so scared of her that they even brought back the corn they'd nicked from the year before.

'Or my mother-in-law . . . She's a woman in a million!'

My mother-in-law is a big woman. And when I say a big woman, I mean a big woman. Well, for a start, she was born on July 21st, 22nd, and 23rd . . .
She's got a good job down at Heathrow Airport. She kick-starts the Jumbo Jets . . .

Despite the brash exterior, Mike is a remarkably shy character. 'I like nothing better than to get away from everything and everyone, and go out in the country with my two dogs – a three-year-old Jack Russell called Patch, and a Red Setter, Tanzy – and just relax. I don't like crowds.'

He goes fishing and shooting a lot. These are his main relaxations, away from the rigours and worries of professional Tomfoolery.

A skinhead walks up to the station ticket-office. He says: ' 'ere, pal, give us a return ticket?'
The booking clerk says, 'Where to, sir?'
Skinhead, pushing his face closer to the window: 'Back 'ere, you great pillock!'

A little lad in a very cosmopolitan classroom. Behind him is sitting a little coloured boy. The teacher says, 'Tommy, where is Africa?'
The white boy points over his shoulder, and says, 'Well, it can't be very far, Miss, 'cos Sambo here goes home for his dinners.'

A fellow walks into the doctor's surgery.
'Doctor, I can't seem to get on with anyone.'
Doctor: 'Why is that?'
He says, 'I don't know . . . you stinking, fat pig!'

I bought my mother-in-law a chair for Christmas. The only trouble is, she won't let me plug it in!

I was out late one night, and didn't get home until 2 a.m.
The wife was up. 'Where have you been?'
I said, 'I've been out drinking with the boys.'
She said, 'One day I'm going to surprise you. What would you do if you came home one night and found me in bed with another man?'
I said, 'I'd shoot his guide-dog.'

This girl said to her boy-friend, 'Do you believe in free love?'
He said, 'What's the matter wiv you . . .? Of course, I do. Have I ever sent you an invoice?'

A motorway caff, with a sign up: 'Food at Popular Prices!'
I went in, ordered a cup of tea and two ham sandwiches.
The bloke charged me £1-40p.
I said, 'Hey, turn it in. What's the idea? I thought it was food at popular prices?'
The fellow on the till says, 'Well, I like 'em, mate.'

I smoke these new cigarettes. They're called Nelson.
You don't get lung cancer smoking these. You just go blind in one eye!

Two little boys talking. One is Jewish. The other says, 'Hey, Louis, what's nine and five?'
Louis says, 'Are you buying, or selling?'

Two blokes in an asylum. One says, 'Harry, is that clock on the wall right?'
He looks at it, says, 'Yes.'
'Well, what's it doing in here, then?'

A mate of mine had a good job in Ireland. He was a rear gunner on a milk float.

There's a big fire at a hotel, and this little Pakistani is standing out on the balcony 18 storeys up, flames all around him. The fire brigade arrive, hold up a big net, and shout: 'Jump!'
He shouts down, 'Oh no. I'm not jumping. I know you white people. When I jump, you'll pull the net away . . .'

The firemen shout, 'Oh come on, mate. Don't mess about. Jump!'

He shouts back: 'No, no, no. You put the net on the ground first, then I'll jump.'

A hippy was walking along the road with one shoe on. A bloke says to him, 'Hello there, mate. Have you lost a shoe?'
Hippy said, 'No, I found one.'

Twelve skinheads walk into a bar, and one says, 'Thirteen pints!'
The barman says, 'Excuse me, sir, but there's only 12 of you.'
The skinhead says, 'Listen, when I ask for 13 pints, I mean 13 pints. OK?'
So they get 13 pints, and they all walk over to a table where there's a little weedy guy sitting on his own. The big feller says to him, 'Here you are, Dad, have a pint on us. We'd like to buy a pint for a cripple.'
The little man says, 'That's very nice of you, son. But I'm not a cripple.'
The skinhead leader says, 'No, but you will be, mate, if you don't buy the next round.'

My boy is only five years old. But he's a skinhead even at five. The teacher said, 'Johnnie, if you had eight sweets, and I took half of them away from you, what would I have?'
He said, 'A broken arm, Miss.'

In School. Little lad: 'Miss, I aint got no pencil.'
Teacher: 'That's wrong, Charlie. Remember your grammar. "I have no pencil. They have no pencils. We have no pencils." '
The kid said, 'Well, who's got all the flaming pencils then?'

A German prison camp. The prisoners are being drilled. This Nazi Sergeant comes out, and yells: 'I want 200 of you to march up to the parachute tower . . . and zen you must all make ze jump, without any parachutes.'
One little Cockney private says, 'What's the matter with you, mate? Jump without parachutes? We'll all be killed.'
The German says, 'That's nonsense. Only some of you will be killed. It is only a case of mind over matter . . . We do not mind, and you do not matter!'

A woman goes into a chemist shop, and asks: 'Have you got a

bedpan please?'
The assistant says, 'Sorry. Have you tried Boots?'
She says: 'Yes, I have. But it comes through the lace holes.'

Six skinheads in a motorway cafe. They walk up to this table, where a fellow has just ordered a meal. And between them, they just push him aside, eat all his dinner, mop up the plate with his bread, finish off his tea, and hit him over the head with the empty cup. The fellow says nothing, but just gets up and walks out.
The skinhead leader starts laughing, and says to the manager of the Caff: 'See that, mate? Not much of a man, was he?'
The fellow says, 'No. He's not much of a driver either – he's just jumped in his lorry and driven over six motor-bikes out in the car-park.'

A little chap walks into the Motor Show in London. There, on one stand, is Mr. Henry Ford. This fellow goes up to him, and says, 'Excuse me, are you Henry Ford, the big motor tycoon?'
Ford says, 'That's right, sir.'
He said, 'Well, I read in a motoring magazine that you built a car in one minute 35 seconds. Is that right?'
Mr. Ford says, 'Well, as a matter of fact, sir, we have built a car in one minute ten seconds flat.'
The little fellow says, 'Yeah, I know . . . I've got it!'

I see the Italians have got a new tank out, ready for the next war. It's got five reverse gears! And one forward gear – just in case someone comes up behind 'em!

A fellow is playing golf, and he hits the ball up the fairway and over the hill. He doesn't know it, but the ball goes onto the road, hits the driver of a passing bus. The bus crashes into three other cars. In the end, 73 people are killed. Sprawled all over the roadway . . .
The golfer comes marching over the hill, looking for his ball. He shouts to another golfer, 'Hey, mate, seen my ball? A Dunlop No. 3?'
The other fellow said, 'I'll tell you something, mister. Your ball came over the hill, went out onto the road, hit the driver of a bus, he crashed his vehicle into three more cars, and there has been a terrible pile-up. Seventy-three people are dead.'
The first golfer says, 'Oh, no! What should I do?'

The other fellow says, 'Well, next time, you should grip the club a little lower down, and you won't slice the ball!'

A German fellow gets a job as a holiday courier. But he's warned by the boss, 'We don't want any of that Nazi nonsense!' So he's fine for three weeks. Then, one day, he's waiting on the station platform. A party of holidaymakers arrive.
'Good morning, happy holidaymakers,' he yells. 'Please line up in twos. You will then march to the holiday camp. From there, you will march to the dining-room. From there, you will march to the swimming-pool . . . From there, you will march to the Dance Hall . . . and from there you will march through Belgium, France and Holland . . . ! ! !'

In America. A young fellow returns home from his first year in the US Army. And his old Hillbilly pappa is sitting out on the verandah, chipping away at a piece of wood. He said, 'Welcome home, son. What did they teach you to do in the Army then, boy?'
The soldier said, 'It was great Pa. They taught me how to throw a hand-grenade.'
The old man said, 'Oh! How?'
The soldier reaches for his bag, pulls out a grenade, takes the pin out and tosses it down the garden, landing right on top of the lavatory roof. Whoof! The lot is blown sky high.
The old man, still chipping at his piece of wood, says: 'You shouldn't have done that, boy.'
He said, 'Why, Pa?'
'Because,' says the old man, 'Your old Momma was in there . . .'

Two fellows die, and one goes up to Heaven, and the other one goes down to the other place. They both meet up a few weeks later – in Tesco's super-market, high in the sky. The fellow up in Heaven says, 'What's it like down there, Charlie?'
Charlie says, 'Smashing, mate. Couldn't be better. All mod cons. Everything you can possibly want. Pubs, betting shops, birds. Everything is done for you. There's a wonderful community spirit. How about you? What's it like up there?'
He says, 'Terrible. Dead rotten. All day long, I'm skivvying away. Polishing the gates, cleaning the marble floors.'
Charlie says, 'Why's that then?'
He says, ''Cos I'm the only one up here.'

A delegation from the West Indies at No. 10 Downing Street. There was a bit of aggro, a bit of political needle, so one fellow turns to Ted Heath and says, 'We have decided to take the Queen's head off our stamps. We have also decided to take the Queen's head off all our coins, in future. Now what do you think about that?'

Mr. Heath says, 'Well, I'm sorry about this, gentlemen. But seeing as that's how you feel, we'll have to take all your fellows off our jars of jam.'

An Army Recruitment Barracks. One fellow is marched in.

Sergeant: 'Name?'

'Davies.'

Sergeant: 'Occupation?'

'Puff.'

Sergeant: 'Puff? What do you mean Puff?'

'I work in a candle factory, as a tester – puffing out candles to see if they work properly.'

Sergeant: 'Right. Next man forward. Name?'

'Jenkins.'

Sergeant: 'What do you do for an occupation?'

'Puff.'

Sergeant: 'In a candle factory?'

'No, I work in a balloon factory – puffing up the balloons to see if they work.'

Sergeant: 'Next man. Name?'

'McCoy.'

Sergeant: 'What do you do?'

'Puff.'

Sergeant: 'Candles or balloons?'

'Neither, Sergeant . . . I'm the real McCoy!'

A skinhead walks into a motor-car showrooms. He's got a few bob, and he fancies a new car. He says, 'Hey, mush, I'd like a really fast motor car, something that will go. OK?'

Salesman: 'Certainly sir. How about a Triumph? A hundred miles an hour, it will go.'

Skinhead: 'Look, mate. I said something fast, didn't I?'

Salesman: 'Well, how about an E-type Jaguar . . . 130 miles an hour?'

Skinhead: 'I've warned you, matey. Don't mess me about. I want something that can really move. What's the fastest car you've got in the showrooms?'

Salesman: 'Well, a Ferrari, sir. It will do 180 mph.'

Skinhead: 'Is that all? I can run faster than that!'

Salesman: 'Look, sir, if you can run faster than that, I'll give you the car for nothing.'

'Right,' said the skinhead. 'You're on.'

So they organised a race. And the salesman took off in the Ferrari, doing 90 mph. And there was the skinhead, loping just behind him. So the salesman thought 'This is ridiculous, I'll show him'.

He put his foot down, and shot the car up to 130 mph. But the skinhead is still with him, running like the wind.

The salesman now became panic-stricken, so put his foot flat on the floor. The car shot up to 185 mph. Suddenly the skinhead keeled over. The salesman stopped the car, went back, and found the fellow sprawled all over the road, a mass of cuts and bruises, and in his bare feet.

Salesman: 'Look, I'm terribly sorry about this. But I did tell you it was impossible for you to run faster than a Ferrari.'

Skinhead: 'Listen mate, it wasn't the Ferrari that beat me . . . . Have you ever had a blow-out in your plimsolls when you're doing 185 mph?'

Charlie was told by his mate that his wife was having a quiet little affair behind his back. So he goes home early one day from work, dashes upstairs, bursts the door open, and screams: 'Okay, where is he? Where's this man you're having an affair with?'

His wife is in the kitchen. 'I don't know what you're talking about,' she says. 'There's no man here.'

Just then, he hears a car starting up, outside. He looks out the window, and sees this fellow about to drive off. So Charlie picks up the fridge, and hurls it out of the window, right on top of the car. With that, his wife picks up a mallet and hits Charlie over the head. Crash!

He wakes up next day in hospital, with a big head. Charlie is feeling a bit sorry for himself, and he turns to the fellow in the next bed, who looks pretty bad with both arms in splints. 'What's the matter with you?'

This fellow says, 'Well, you won't believe this mate. But I was just driving my car, when some maniac threw a fridge out of a third-storey window, and it landed right on top of my car.'

Charlie thought 'Oh hell!' Then he sees a fellow further down the ward, absolutely swathed in bandages from head to foot.

'What's up with you, then, mate?' he asks.
This geezer peers through the slits in his bandages, and says,
'Well, I was sitting in this fridge . . .'

Bernard Manning is so mean, he drinks whisky and Horlicks
together. When it's his turn to pay, he's always fast asleep!

Chapter Thirteen
BRYN PHILLIPS

BRYN PHILLIPS, the good looking fellow from South Wales, was always given the 'idiot' parts in the school plays as a lad. So it was not surprising, perhaps, that he should turn out to be a professional comedian.

But his early life was no laughing matter for Bryn. He was born and brought up in the little mining village of Abercynon, Glamorgan, where life wasn't easy. He was an only child, and with his father away in the war and his mother going out to work, he was brought up largely by his grandmother.

When he left school, his first job lasted exactly four hours. He fancied himself as a tailor. 'But I was put in with a lot of old women, sewing buttons on jackets, and I couldn't stick it. So I walked out the first day,' recalls Bryn.

Because jobs were hard to come by, he went down the mines, much against the advice of his mother. But when he had an accident – a water pump fell on his foot – his mother insisted that he pack the coal-mining job in after only six months, with the warning: 'Your Uncle Charlie broke his back in the pits.' After that, he worked as a fireman on the Railways.

After two years National Service in the Welsh Guards, he

returned to Civvy Street in Wales, and went into the fruit-and-veg business, with his father, later branching out on his own.

It was here that he first started to find an interest in comedy. 'There was nothing very amusing about selling vegetables, so I started playing in pubs and clubs around South Wales, trying my hand as a comedian.' He teamed up with another handsome young Welshman called Tommy Woodward, who was regarded locally as a pretty good singer.

They played the clubs together for some time, Bryn doing comedy and Tommy singing. The partnership split up when Woodward hit the Big Time and moved to London – and changed his name to Tom Jones.

'We had some great fun together,' says Bryn. 'We used to pick up about seven-and-sixpence a night each for playing the clubs. But as long as they gave us a few pints of beer as well, we were happy.

'One night, I remember, we were paid off for a night's work with a tin of salmon apiece. Salmon was a bit of a luxury in the Welsh valleys in those days, and it seemed at the time to be quite a good pay-off.'

Both Tom and Bryn were married very young. Bryn's wife Marjorie came from Dulwich, but moved to Wales with her parents during the war.

Shortly after Tom Jones moved to the bright lights of London to earn his fortune, Bryn decided to turn full-time comedian. 'I was tired of fruit and vegetables . . . I was also near to bankruptcy,' he says. 'I just went to all my debtors and asked them for time to pay.'

The bright lights – plus the success of Tom Jones – greatly appealed to him, and Bryn was determined to get away from the fruit business. 'I used to run a van for buying and selling veg and fish during the day, and we also used the van for travelling around as a pop group, and for carrying the musical instruments to clubs at night.

'The van used to stink of fish, but there would be six or seven of us, all with our best stage suits on. And by the end of the week, we'd all stink as much as the fish.'

His entry into professional show business, however, was not auspicious. He found himself at Blackpool, doing 28 shows in a week for £35. Then, when he went to Manchester to play for the first time, he walked into a club and found an audience of nearly 1,000 men. What he didn't know was that it was a 'stag' night, and the audience expected dirty jokes.

112

Bryn went in and asked for his dressing-room. Someone pointed to a door. He walked in – and found six beautiful girls in varying state of undress, some completely nude.

'Oh, excuse me,' he stammered, 'I'm the comic, and I'm looking for my dressing-room.' One of the girls said, 'Yes, this is it – that's you over there', and she pointed to a coat hanger in one corner of the room.

'I had to share this large dressing-room with all the girls,' Bryn chuckles. 'It was so embarrassing . . . I didn't know where to look – first!'

Then, when he went out on stage, the men in the audience banged their pint pots on the tables and shouted 'Off! Off!' Not, this time at the girls, but at Bryn. Because his jokes were too clean!

'I didn't have a clue about stag clubs, and I had never even seen a strip show before,' says Bryn. 'I died on stage that night. I came off in tears. It was an awful experience. Terrible.

'But in those days, I'm afraid that comedians had to do stag shows – or starve. I got £2 10s. a night.'

Bryn also appeared in fellow comedian Bernard Manning's club, in his early days in Manchester. 'I didn't go down very well, and I begged Bernard to pay me off before the week was through, but he wouldn't,' says Bryn.

'Audiences in Manchester can be tough on strangers – particularly foreigners, like the Welsh. Once they accept you, however, they're great.'

He had not appeared on TV at all, before his chance came in *The Comedians*. He was immediately put on a long-term contract after his first TV taping.

Bryn has sometimes been accused of being too good looking for a comic. 'When I used to walk out, audiences expected me to sing. They were disappointed, I often felt, when I started coming out with gags – particularly "blue" ones.'

He's been a lifelong fan of Jerry Lewis, and always wanted to be a visual comedian. ('As a kid, I would stand in front of the mirror and practise pulling funny faces – until my parents were both convinced I was going mad.')

He has also had to soften his thick Welsh accent a little. He admits he's died on stage many times. Even in Wales, he's 'Dai-d'! 'But the TV show has made up for a whole lot of early disappointments in my career,' he says.

Now married, with a family of four boys – Paul, Michael, Christopher and Bryn – he still lives in his beloved South Wales, although his work now involves him in a great deal of travel, all over the country.

His success in show business has undoubtedly given his parents, who are both physically handicapped, a great deal of satisfaction. And Bryn still lives with his family near to his parents.

When he looks at those stark pit heads, and sees the miners going underground, he knows just what he has escaped from. 'I suppose I've been lucky,' he says.

There's a fellow lives next door to me who sprays his lawn with pink gin . . . so that the grass will come up half cut!

I've another neighbour who never works. He went to the Labour Exchange. They said, 'What's your occupation?'
He said, 'I'm a Zeppelin maker.'

This fellow is so lazy . . . His wife said to him: 'Go out and see if it's raining?'
He said, 'Why not bring the dog in, and see if it's wet?'

An actor was offered £2,000 a week to work on a new film.
'That's good pay,' he said, 'What's the film?'
The director said, ' "Long John Silver" and you've got the title role. We start shooting the film on Tuesday.'
The actor said, 'Why can't we start on Monday?'
Director: 'Because on Monday, you'll be in hospital, having your leg off.'

There was a knock on Charlie's door. A fellow was standing on the doorstep. 'I'm collecting for Dr. Barnardo's Home', he said. So Charlie gave him five of his kids.

A little Welsh chap in London, awed by the big city. He fancied an Indian meal. Walking down Oxford Street, he saw a shop with the sign: 'Curry's'. He went in – and they sold him a bike!

Two beatniks walking down the street when they saw a plane overhead. Suddenly, it went on fire, and they saw the pilot eject himself out of the plane. One turned to the other and said, 'Man, dig that crazy toaster!'

Two coloured fellows were sitting on the sands at Torquay, trying to get sun-burned! Dai fancied a swim, so he said to these two chaps: 'What's the water like?'
One coloured chappie said: 'It luke warm.'
So Dai went in . . . and came out three minutes later looking like a biro refill. He was frozen stiff. He said, 'I thought you said it was luke warm?'
The big black fellow said, 'Well, it looked warm to me.'

I was driving down a country lane. And I stopped and knocked at this farmer's door. I told him, 'Excuse me, but six of your chickens are no longer laying.'
The farmer said, 'How do you know?'
I said, 'I've just run over them.'

A dear little old Welsh woman was at the seaside. She saw the men preparing to go fishing, collecting their baskets and nets. She said to one of them: 'What are those things?'
He said, 'Lobster pots.'
She said, 'Go on, you'll never train them to sit on those things!'

I took the wife on holiday, and she was rushed to hospital, a month before we expected her to be, to have a baby. I was pacing up and down the corridor, waiting for news. I said to this fellow, sitting there: 'What a thing to happen! I'm on holiday!'
This fellow turned round, and said: 'You should worry, mate! I'm only on my honeymoon!'

My friend Dai is so mean. He was out playing golf, and he had his little niece walking around with him. They were just coming up to the seventh, and she said, 'Oh, Uncle Dai, it's my birthday. What are you going to give me?'
He said, 'I'll give you the next two holes.'

A Pakistani driver got a job on the buses in Manchester. One of those one-man buses, he'd never even seen before. They told him, 'It's quite simple. You collect the fares . . . then off you go!'
First day out, he ends up crashing the bus straight through a plate-glass window of a shop. The Inspector rushes round to the accident. The Pakistani is sitting there, among the debris. They asked him: 'Abdul, what happened?'
He said, 'I don't know . . . I was upstairs collecting the fares.'

Have you seen the latest machine in the fairgrounds? You put a shilling in and ask it any question, and it gives you a true answer. I tried it last week. I asked the machine: 'Where is my father? The machine replied: 'Your father is fishing off Wigan Pier.'
Well, I thought, that's daft for a start, because my father is dead. So I put another shilling in, and asked it another question: 'OK, let's try you again . . . Where's my mother's husband?'
The machine boomed out: 'Your mother's husband is buried in South Wales . . . but your father is still fishing off Wigan Pier!'

An Irish man was up in court for not paying maintenance to his wife. The judge said, 'You should be ashamed of yourself, Murphy. I'm awarding your wife £5 a week.'
Murphy said, 'That's very good of you, sir, and I'll try and send her a few bob myself.'

A fellow was fighting to get on the bus. And this little Indian conductor was trying to keep him off. He shouted: 'You cannot get on this bus. Me crammed jam full.'
The fellow said, 'I don't care what your name is, mate . . . I'm coming on.'

Three fellows were in court for being drunk and disorderly. They were all unfortunately cross-eyed, and to add to their problems the magistrate was cross-eyed, as well.
So there were these three cross-eyed fellows in the dock, and a cross-eyed magistrate on the bench.
The magistrate looked at the first fellow, and said, 'What's your name?'
The second fellow said, 'Smith.'
The magistrate said, 'I wasn't talking to you.'
And the third fellow said, 'I never said a word.'

Two old folk live next door to me. He's 97 and she's 95. But they're so independent. Last Sunday, Mrs. Jones was down the bottom of the garden, cutting a cabbage for dinner. But she suddenly fainted, and went out like a light. Flat out, she was.
Mr. Jones came dashing out, and struggled to pick her up. I said: 'Can you manage?'
Mr. Jones said, 'Oh aye, I'll manage. I'll open a tin of peas.'

Dai came home from work early one night, and his wife Blodwen had another fellow with her – another coal-miner who had come straight off the afternoon shift, and was as black as Jomo Kenyatta. As soon as she heard Dai's key in the door, she said, 'Quick, you'd better hide.' So the boy-friend went and hid.

Dai came in, and said, 'I'm feeling a bit peckish, I think I'll make myself a cheese sandwich.' He opened the fridge, and there was this little black fellow.

The fellow said, 'You ain't gonna believe this, but I've just fallen off the label on the jar of jam on the top shelf.'

My mate Dai holds the record in the coal mines. He's the only fellow who has done 100 yards in his pit boots . . . He fell down a lift shaft.

I saw a massive funeral in Moss Side, Manchester. With 14,000 Pakistanis and 16,000 West Indians walking behind the hearse. I tapped one fellow on the shoulder, and said: 'Who's dead?'
He said, 'The bloke in the front coach.'
I said, 'Yes, but he must have been a pretty important man?'
He said: 'He was. He was the National Assistance Officer.'

Chapter Fourteen
SYD FRANCIS

SYD FRANCIS is a miserable so-and-so. And he's the first to admit it. 'I would never have been a comic if it hadn't been for a sore lip,' he says, pathetically.

He comes from Blackpool, and started out in show business as a child prodigy, billed as 'Britain's Wonder Boy Trumpeter!' He used to tour the No. 2 music halls with his Uncle Syd, a bass player, looking after him. Each town he played, he went to a different school, working at night in the theatre. His father, Jack Walmsley, was a dance-band singer.

Syd had his first summer season at the age of 12, at the North Pier, Blackpool. 'I got £50 a week. Fantastic money in those days!'

Then, with music halls closing down, he went to Germany with his trumpet act and carried on working. Seven years ago, he was back here, playing the Ba Ba Club in Barnsley, when he found he couldn't hit the right notes because of a cold on his lip.

'I was expected to do a 40-minute spot. But halfway through, I just stopped and apologised to the audience. "You must excuse me, but I can't go on. My lips hurt and I can't play properly." '

The audience roared with laughter. Syd went on: 'You know,

this sort of thing is always happening to me. I'm dead unlucky.'
And he went on chatting about his experiences in show business.
And the more he told them about his troubles, the more the
audience laughed. They quickly warmed to his soft Lancashire
drawl, and his dead-pan face and winsome appeal.

'I didn't tell any jokes. I didn't have to. They just laughed at
my own experiences,' he recalls.

What did he tell them about? 'Well, about getting my first big
break in Blackpool. And then being introduced to a big-time
impresario and song-writer who offered me a contract. But
before I could sign it, he died.

'Then I did a deal with another agent – but within a week he
was dead, too.'

He then went on a variety tour and managed to get a spot in
a radio programme from Manchester. 'I told fifty agents and
important show business people to listen,' he says. 'In the
middle of the programme, there was a four-bar introduction
from the orchestra and I was supposed to do my spot. But at
that precise time, they interrupted the show for a gale warning
. . . and I was never heard by anyone!'

After that first season at Blackpool, he was offered a show in
Glasgow. The contract was signed, but then someone discovered
Syd was under 15. Under local regulations, this barred him from
appearing.

He then lost the chance of an appearance on the Ed Sullivan
Show in America because he was too young. 'I had a cable from
Mr. Sullivan offering me an appearance on his coast-to-coast US
programme, but when he learned I wasn't yet fifteen, they
dropped the invitation.'

Syd now makes a great play out of being so unlucky. 'I just
tell audiences that I regard myself as the unluckiest chap alive,
and they all sympathise with me.' It's his dry, mournful style
which wins Syd some of his biggest laughs.

Now, he spices his tales of woe with standard one-liners . . .

Even if I buy Treets, they melt in my hand . . .
*If I was born a triplet to Raquel Welch, I'd be the one on the
bottle . . .*
If I fought a duel . . . I'd come third.

When he's going well with an audience, he will stop and
thank them.

'I don't usually get such a nice audience. They usually walk
out when I come on. Not that I mind. I only begin to worry

when they walk towards me!

'But I can often go twenty minutes without telling a single gag,' he says. He never smiles, either. 'I don't see anything funny to laugh at!'

In 1969, he won an award from *The Stage* trade paper – for his musical speciality act. He still considers himself a trumpeter, not a comedian.

His wife Judy is pretty hot stuff. She has a fire-eating act, and performs under the name of Judy Allen. They try to work on the same bill as often as possible, and their five-year-old son Andrew can already play the trumpet.

Ken Goodwin is one of Syd's closest chums. 'We started out together,' Syd recalls. 'That was long before Ken started laughing at his own jokes, and I started to be so unlucky.'

On one occasion, they both found themselves at Wigan. A club secretary said he could offer one of them a date for the following Friday – at £12. 'So we both went – for six quid each,' says Syd. 'Ken and I shared the booking.'

Syd was unlucky again, when he was asked to do a contribution to Granada's programme on Ken Goodwin, screened early in 1972. He'd worked out a quick sketch with Goodwin at Blackpool, where they both appeared last summer. But the whole thing went wrong, and Syd's final contribution to the Goodwin programme was cut out altogether.

In the sketch, Syd was supposed to be playing a post horn on the jetty, and Ken would come along, and they would both run away when they heard the sound of barking hounds. But disaster! The mouthpiece of Syd's horn fell through a crack in the landing-stage and into the sea below.

He needed the mouthpiece for his act that night, so he telephoned the coastguards, found the tide would be out just fifteen minutes before he was due on stage. So he had his wife, son, mother and a half-a-dozen passers-by out on the sands as the tide went out, looking for his mouthpiece.

They never found it. The tide went out on time – but only on either side of the pier. Beneath the pier, a deep stream remained – with his musical mouthpiece still somewhere submerged.

That night, Syd went on stage and told the audience he was the unluckiest man in the world, and reeled off just what had happened earlier in the day. They roared with laughter.

'It's a pity everybody laughs at me,' says Syd. 'I don't want to be a funny-man. I'd much rather be a good trumpeter. Like I said, I'm just dead unlucky!'

I recently bought a new suit, and paid extra for two pairs of trousers . . . Then I burnt a hole in the jacket!

I went for a driving test last week. On my way there, I ran over the examiner.

I've got a bad back . . . I fell off the ladder when I was ironing the curtains!

On my holidays last year in Spain, I saw this notice: 'Topless Bar'.
I thought that's for me. I went in . . . and it was a cafe with no roof on!

You sit outside to have your meal in those open-air cafes.
First time I went in one, it rained . . . It took me an hour to finish my soup.

I said to the doctor: 'I think I'm suffering from an inferiority complex.'
The doctor said: 'It's not a complex. You're just inferior.'

We lost my Dad when we were on holiday. I went to the police station with my Mum, and the officer said, 'What does he look like?'
She said, 'He's tall, dark, good-looking, something like Gregory Peck, and he's very athletic.'
I said, 'Hold on, Mam. Dad's nothing like that.'
She said, 'I know, but who the hell wants him back?'

We found out my Dad was in an accident. He got run over by a steam-roller. I went into hospital to visit him. I said, 'Which ward is he in?'
The nurse replied, 'He's in Wards 8, 9, and 10.'

My Dad's coming home next week. My Mam has left a note next door . . . 'Just in case I'm out, will you slip him under the door?'

I really am terribly unlucky, though . . . If I buy Polo mints, the hole is always on the outside!

My bad luck started when I was a child . . . My Dad bought me

a rocking-horse for my birthday . . . and it died!
An Uncle then gave me a pet duck . . . and it sank!

I got a letter last week from the solicitors, telling me an Uncle had left me a chain of barbers' shops . . . in Vietnam.

I was in Blackpool all last summer. Everyone else got sunburned . . . I just got pneumonia.

A gorilla went into this pub, put a pound on the counter and asked for a pint of beer. So the barman gave him a pint, but he gave him only 50 pence change. The barman said, 'I hope you don't mind me staring at you, but we don't get many gorillas in here.'
The gorilla looked up from his pint, and said, 'It's not surprising, mate, at ten bob a pint for bitter!'

People in London think Northerners are all stupid. They think we're dense, don't they? I don't know why. I read in the paper the other day that the population in London was the densest in the whole country.

I was playing Bingo for the first time. I had most of my card filled in, with only number-13 to go. The Bingo caller picked up another ball and shouted: 'The next number is . . . unlucky for some.' . . .
So I jumped up and yelled 'Bingo!'
And he announced the number: 'Twelve!'
I said, 'Hey, 12 is not an unlucky number.'
He said, 'It is for you, mate.'

. . . Even my Mam and Dad were unlucky . . . They had me!

Chapter Fifteen
DAVE BUTLER

DAVE BUTLER is the comic who brings a touch of the West Country to *The Comedians*. He comes from Bristol and served his apprenticeship as an entertainer by following in the footsteps of people like Dave Allen, Des O'Connor, as a Butlin redcoat.

'I did the lot,' he says. 'Everything from announcing the day's events in the dining-hall, to dancing with the old-age pensioners at night.'

But Dave also took part in the nightly camp concerts. He did an act, miming to the records of such stars as Spike Jones and Stan Freberg.

He started with Butlin's when he was 21 and worked as a redcoat at Ayr, Pwllheli and Clacton-on-Sea. 'It was at Clacton,' he recalls, 'back in 1963, that someone pinched my tape-recorder. I was completely lost, but I still had to go on stage and entertain the holidaymakers, somehow. So I strolled on, to the accompaniment of my knees knocking, and just told some jokes.'

From that moment, he decided he didn't need to buy a new tape-recorder. He would make his way as a solo comedian in his own right. No more miming to other stars' voices.

There was plenty of variety in his life, before he went full-time into show business. He left school at 15 and joined a butcher, then he switched to become an engineering apprentice, joined the RAF at 17 only to be discharged after two weeks. So he went back to butchering . . . but quit after a couple of years to become a commercial traveller.

(His fellow comics insist that Dave was fired from the Butcher's shop. They say he was working the bacon slicer one day when the manager sat on the machine by mistake . . . and everyone got a little behind with their orders!)

Dave's next job was travelling around hardware stores, getting orders for Domestos, Stergene and Squezy. ('That didn't last long. The job drove me round the bend').

His first professional dates as a stand-up comic were in the Manchester area, when he received twenty-five shillings a night. 'Just enough to keep me alive – even if I did die on my feet most nights!'

In 1968 came his big break. He was invited back to Butlin's – but with a difference. This time he returned as resident comic with a summer company playing at Filey. He was booked solely as an entertainer. His redcoat days were over. No more dancing with the old-age pensioners!

Further summer seasons followed at Butlin's in Skegness and, last summer, at Bognor. 'I was all set to go back to a holiday camp this summer,' says Dave. 'But when the offer of a summer season with the stage version of *The Comedians* came along, and then a season at the London Palladium, I was very kindly released from a previous contract. I still can't really believe I've played the London Palladium!'

Dave has now adapted his style of comedy so that he gives a West Country slant to most of his jokes.

A farmer of 83 married a girl of 22. He couldn't keep his hands off her – so he sacked his hands, and bought a combine harvester!

A fellow went looking for a job down on a farm. He said to the farmer, 'Can you use me on the land?'
The farmer said, 'No, we've got special stuff for that!'

An American, visiting the West Country, came across a typical yokel. 'Do you have a village idiot?' he asked.
'No,' said the yokel. 'We take it in turns.'

He gets most of his gags, he says, from professional writers ('I buy them in batches, and I've paid as much as £10 for a few jokes and never used a line, because the jokes couldn't be adapted to suit my style').

His favourite comic, he says, is Benny Hill, because of his tremendous versatility. Dave owes a lot, too, to Bob Monkhouse. 'It was Bob who got me the job of warming-up the studio audience on *The Golden Shot* TV programme, in Birmingham, a couple of years ago.'

For his stage act, Dave has a standard opening . . . 'I was going to start with my latest record – it's called *I Love You* on the front side, and *Kiss Me* on the backside . . .'

Newly-wed Dave now lives with his wife Christine in Blackpool. 'I met her at a club in Wigan,' he says. 'No one was laughing at my jokes – except Christine. I think she just felt rather sorry for me.' ('I do a lot of travelling in this business. With my act, I've got to keep on the move!')

I went to a farmer, and I asked him: 'Got any odd jobs?'
He said, 'Yes, you can go and try milking the bull.'

A fellow walked into work late. The foreman said, 'You should have clocked on at two o'clock. It's now three. Where have you been?'
This bloke said, 'I've been to have my hair cut.'
Foreman: 'In the firm's time?'
He said, 'Well, it grows in the firm's time, doesn't it?'
The foreman said, 'Yes, but it doesn't all grow in the firm's time, does it?'
He said, 'Well, I didn't have it all cut off.'

There's a lunatic asylum near us. I phoned them up the other day. A fellow answered the phone. I said, 'Is that the lunatic asylum?'
He said, 'Yes, but we're not on the phone! Sorry.'

I come from the West Country, from a little place called Wedlock.
Well, I was born just outside it actually!

A fellow was complaining to the butcher the other day. He said, 'My wife bought a piece of mutton. It was that big. She put it in the oven, and it shrivelled up to half the size.'
The butcher said, 'That's funny. Last week, my wife bought a woolly jumper that big, she washed it once and it shrivelled down to half the size . . . It must have been off the same sheep.'

I used to work down on the farm. I was a pilot . . .
I used to pile it over here, and pile it over there!

A fellow I know had only one knee. The doctor examined him, and said, 'You'll have to go to Africa – because that's where the knee-grows!'
So he went to the African jungle and he came across an ape who had no knees at all. He took the animal to a witch doctor to see if he could get two ape-knees for a penny!

I went to the doctor's this morning. Couldn't go last week, I was ill. . . .
A fellow there said to the doctor: 'Can I have some more sleeping tablets for the wife?'
The doctor said, 'Why?'
He said, 'She's woken up.'

Another fellow was in the doctor's. He walked in to be examined.
'Doctor, I keep losing my temper.'
Doctor: 'I beg your pardon?'
He snapped: 'I told you once, you fool . . . !'

A fellow tried crossing a chicken with an octopus, thinking he might get a chicken with eight legs. He succeeded, too. The only trouble is, he's now got sixteen chickens each with eight legs . . . but he can't catch any of them.

A lady came into the surgery. She said, Doctor, every time I sneeze I get passionate. What should I take for it?'
He said, 'Snuff.'

A fellow complained to the Doctor: 'I've swallowed a peanut, and it's stuck in my throat.'
The Doctor said, 'Don't panic. Just go home, drink a gallon of hot chocolate, and the peanut will come out a Treet.'

I was on board a boat coming from Ireland to Liverpool.

Suddenly there was a shout, 'Man overboard!' The Captain shouted, 'Throw in a buoy.' So this Irishman standing next to me grabbed a little lad aged about eight and flung him overboard into the sea.
The Captain said, 'No, you fool. I meant a cork buoy.'
The Irishman said, 'Well, in an emergency like this, how the hell am I to know which part of Ireland he comes from?'

I saw my next-door neighbour the other day. He was doing a bit of carpentry in the back garden. I said to him, 'How's the wife?'
He said, 'She's not very well.'
I said, 'Oh dear, is that her coughin'?'
He said, 'No, I'm just making a rocking-horse for the kids.'

A fellow at the bus stop. He had no arms and no legs.
The bloke behind him said, 'How are you getting on?'

A fellow went to the Doctor's. The Doctor said, 'I've got some good news for you. You'll be pleased to know that the operation you had for deafness has been a complete success.'
The fellow said, 'What?'

A pal of mine got engaged and he said to his girl-friend, 'Darling I've got a confession to make – I'm colour blind.'
She said, 'Well, I can't marry you', and off she went.
He met another girl six months later, got engaged, and told her the same thing. 'I'm sorry, but I'm colour blind.'
She said, 'Let's call the whole thing off'. And she left him.
He thought 'The next time I won't tell her, until afterwards.'
And he met another girl soon afterwards, got married, and a week after the wedding, he told her: 'Darling, I've got a little confession to make – I'm colour blind.'
And this big darkie bird said, 'Yo sure am, honey-child. Yo sure am.'

A woman in the Grocer's shop.
'Can I have a bottle of sauce?'
Grocer: 'Certainly. H.P.?'
She said, 'No, I'll pay for it now.'

A mouse went into a music shop, and asked: 'Have you got a mouse-organ, please?'

The fellow behind the counter said, 'That's very funny. You're the second mouse that's been in here this morning asking for a mouse-organ.'

The mouse said, 'Oh, that must have been our Monica!'

I know a fellow who crossed a seagull with a parrot. Now he's got a bird that flies up and down Blackpool promenade in the summer, apologising to the holidaymakers.

A fellow bought a budgie from the pet-shop. He said, 'I'd like one that sings, please.' So he got a nice budgie, took it home, and it warbled away all week.

Then, this fellow suddenly noticed the following Friday that the budgie had only one leg. So back he goes to the pet-shop, and he says: 'Hey, this budgie you sold me has only got one leg.'

The shop-keeper said, 'You asked for a singer, mate. Not a tap-dancer.'

Chapter Sixteen
SAMMY THOMAS

SAMMY THOMAS is a pretty hard character. They call him the Chocolate Smarty. He's been peddling his particular brand of black comedy longer than anyone else. It was he, in fact, who first started the trend towards telling racial jokes aimed at his own colour.

Now, his act is sprinkled with references to Darkies, Sambos, Coons and Niggers. 'Prejudice will never be stamped out – it's like prostitution,' he says earnestly. But he insists that his colour helps him enormously with his act. 'I find that being coloured is a big asset in this business.'

I'm not colour prejudiced . . . Why, even some of my friends are black.

Sammy was born in Manchester, but now lives in Doncaster. His father was a Nigerian, his mother a Lancashire woman. For ten years he worked as a draughtsman. His decision to turn comedian came the night he attended a business dinner, and the cabaret artist failed to turn up.

So Sammy got up and told a few jokes, just to pass the time.

131

Everyone applauded, and he found himself the star turn of the night.

After that, he set about the task of studying and collecting jokes. And from there, developed a completely new show business career as an entertainer.

He has a slight lisp which he also uses to great advantage, for this makes his style of telling gags even funnier.

Most of his comedy is pure tongue-in-cheek.

Jomo Kenyatta met President Nkrumah, and said, 'Now there's a fellow with a funny name – Ian Smith'.

There are two things I hate – colour prejudice and darkies ...
I used to work in the Post Office. I was a black-mailer.

'For a long time, TV producers were afraid of me and my kind of racial material,' says Sammy. 'They wouldn't touch me.'

Now he has proved, along with Charlie Williams and Jos White, on *The Comedians*, that they can get laughs at their own expense, by poking fun at the coloured man.

'When I tell jokes about the coloured man I'm really hitting at the white man and his ridiculous prejudices,' says Sammy.

('I used to work down the mines. But they fired me ... because they could never find me.')

He is a good deal more abrasive than either Williams or White. More sardonic. More biting. More vicious. 'But I'm never really vindictive,' he says.

He likes to 'have a go' at his audiences, to get them riled. To a consistent heckler, he will say uncompromisingly, 'It's a pity your mother wasn't on the pill.'

Sammy is married and has a family of four. He dresses immaculately, always has a big cigar during his act, and prides himself on being one of the best ad-libbers in the business.

('You know Enoch Powell's signature tune ... *I'm Just Mad About Sammy!*')

I don't perspire – they call it coondensation!

I went into a Manchester hotel and was walking through reception.
The man behind the desk said, 'Excuse me, sir, have you got a reservation?'
I said, 'What do you think I am, a ruddy Red Indian?'

This Pakistani wanted to make a political protest. So he covered himself from head to toe in petrol, put a match to himself – and very quickly died. Just as a protest.
There were big headlines in the papers. Now everyone in the district is collecting for his wife and relatives. Up to last night, they'd collected 96 gallons of petrol!

George Roper is a lovely fellow. He always invites me home whenever I'm in Manchester . . . just so that his kids can chalk on me!

A black man died and went up to Heaven. He was met by St. Peter who said, 'We don't normally allow coloured people in here – not unless they've done something special in life.'
'I have,' said the black man, 'I'm the most courageous cat you've ever seen. How about this? I married a white woman in a white man's church in Alabama, USA, and there were 50 Klu Klux Klan in the congregation.'
St. Peter said, 'That's fantastic. When was that?'
The darky said, 'Two minutes ago.'

A Pakistani moved in next door to a posh city gent. After a couple of days, he popped his head over the garden fence and said to the white man, 'I've got exactly the same house as you, so I'm as good as you are.'
The white man, trying to be nice to him, said, 'Yes, of course you are.'
A week later, the darky buys a new car, pops his head over the fence and says: 'I've got exactly the same house as you, and now I've got exactly the same car as you, so I'm as good as you are.'
The white man says, 'Yes, of course you are, old boy.'
Next day, the darky stops the white man on his way out, and says: 'Listen, I've been thinking. I'm even better off than you are.'
'Now wait a minute,' says the business gent. 'How do you make

133

that out?'

'Well, I've got exactly the same house as you, I've got exactly the same car as you . . . But I aint got no ruddy Pakistani living next door to me!'

I was driving along when I crossed a white line. A police car came after me. The officer said, 'I'm going to book you for crossing a white line and also for speeding. Let's have a look at your Wog Book.'

In the year 2001, we'll have black and white TV sets and coloured engineers . . . And we'll have the Christmas Day broadcast from Buckingham Palace over the radio: 'Good afternoon, cats. Dis is yo Queen speakin'.'

Enoch Powell has brought out a new pamphlet. It's called 'How To Get Rid Of Black Heads.'

Six coloured fellows on the roads, digging a big hole, and this Irish labourer driving a steamroller, backed it up, and flattened them all into the ground. He thought he was going to get the sack. Instead, they gave him a rise in pay . . . It was the first time anyone had ever tar-laid a road, and put in the cat's eyes at the same time!

You've never seen a coloured comedian on the BBC, have you? BBC – it stands for Ban Black Comics!

This Jewish gentleman was waiting at the bus stop. Next to him was a little coloured chap. The coloured fellow said, 'What time's the next bus due?'

The Jew said, 'Half past ten, you black sod.'

Chapter Seventeen
ALAN FOX

ALAN FOX, curly-haired, bespectacled, was a shipyard worker at South Shields, County Durham, and doing odd gigs as a vocalist when he appeared on a London charity show with Frankie Vaughan. This gave him the taste for big-time show business.

A 'teenage member of the Tyne Dock Youth Club, he was encouraged by the warden, Ernie Wales, to develop as an entertainer. And when Frankie Vaughan visited the club during a nationwide tour of youth clubs, he heard Alan sing and was impressed with the lad. Alan's act then included impressions of artists like Slim Whitman, Johnnie Ray, and Frankie Vaughan himself.

On the strength of this, Frank took him to a youth club charity concert, called *Clubs Are Trumps*, at the Festival Hall, London. Meeting well-known artists such as Vera Lynn, the late Alma Cogan and Billy Cotton made Alan think seriously about the possibilities of going into show business himself. But the government decided that the country's need for Mr. Fox's services was greater than that of show business . . . and he was called up on National Service.

Transferred from the Durham Light Infantry, because they

discovered he was colour blind, he finished up as a bombardier drill-instructor at Oswestry with the Royal Artillery.

It was at Oswestry that he started doing shows with the camp concert party. ('But I could never do much singing, because I was always hoarse with all the shouting on the barrack square').

After Army service, Alan went back to working in the ship-yard, as a boilermaker. ('I'm still a fully-fledged boilermaker,' he says. 'If things ever get tough, I can always go back to using a blow-lamp').

He gave this up, however, to try his hand as a salesman in a tailor's shop. In the evenings, he started entertaining as a singer, going in for what were known as 'Go As You Please' contests. 'I could pick up thirty bob if I won one of these talent shows. I also used to enter contests at lunch-time shows over the week-end, sometimes picking up as much as three pounds a time.'

In 1960, he turned professional, as a singer. The gags gradually caught up on him. 'I started by just telling the odd joke in between my songs. But then, one night, a couple of pals in show business told me I should concentrate more on the comedy side of my act. So I did.'

For the past five years, he's earned something of a reputation up North as a fast, staccato-type comic.

Alan is a newcomer, this year, to *The Comedians*. He owes his TV chance to topping the bill last summer at the Casino Rooms, Douglas, Isle of Man. Showman Peter Webster saw his act and suggested to producer Johnnie Hamp that he should give Fox a try-out. He was first invited to the studios last September, recorded some material, and finally made his TV debut in February 1972.

Alan (real name: Thomas Duffy) is married and has two children, Janet and Kevin.

My son came up to me the other day, and said 'Give me ten-pence and I'll tell you a secret.'

I said: 'What's the secret?'

He said, 'I'll tell you who sleeps with Mummy when you're away.'

So I gave him ten-pence, and said, 'Who?'

He ran off with the money, and said, 'It's me!'

'I love kids,' says Alan. 'I used to be one, myself, when I was young!'

The fellow next door to me is always drunk. Funny thing is, his wife didn't even know he drank – until one night he came home sober, and his dog attacked him.

He was staggering home one night, when he was stopped by a policeman. The copper said, 'What's your name?'
He said, 'Duncan.'
The officer asked, 'Duncan what?'
He said, 'Duncan Disorderley, what are you going to do about it?'

An Englishman, an Irishman and a Scotsman went on a cruise together. The liner suddenly struck a reef and started to sink. 'We'd better do something religious,' said the Englishman. So the Englishman started to sing hymns; the Irishman said his prayers; and the Scotsman took a collection!

I did my bit in the Forces, you know. Oh yes! I was in Cyprus when the first bullet was fired. . . . I was in Newcastle when the second bullet was fired!

One fellow I knew didn't want to join up. He went for a medical and he said, 'You can't take me in the Army.'
The MO said, 'Why not?'
He said, 'I've got one leg shorter than the other.'
The officer said, 'So what? The ground won't be level where you're fighting . . . you're in!'

Another fellow said, 'I'm no good for the Army. I'm bad with my nerves. If anyone shouts at me, I jump.'
The sergeant shouted: 'Right. Paratroopers!'

This drunk was staggering home one night when he got knocked down by a bus. He picked himself up, stepped right into the traffic again, and got knocked down by a bike. He got up and started complaining.
The fellow on the bike said, 'It's your own fault. You should walk down the street – there's a Zebra crossing.'
This drunk said, 'Is there? Well, I hope he's having better luck getting across this road than I am.'

He was staggering down the road, another night, with a half bottle of whisky in his back pocket. He slipped over, and heard a crash. He just lay there, then felt a trickle down his legs. He looked up to Heaven, and said, 'Please, Lord, make that blood!'

Robin Hood was dying in a little cottage deep in the heart of Sherwood Forest. His strength was weakening, so he said, 'Bring me my bow and arrow, and open the window.'

So Little John did this. Robin said, 'I will fire this arrow, and wherever it lands, I want you to bury me there.'

He took aim – and he fired. And Little John and his other outlaw friends stuck to Robin's last dying wish . . . they buried him on top of the wardrobe!

A fellow went for an interview for a job down the mines.

The boss said, 'Do you know anything about working down a pit?'

He said, 'Yes, I do.'

The boss said, 'Do you know your gas regulations?'

He said, 'Oh aye. Well, I know it's Mark 7 for Yorkshire puddings.'

Did you hear about the woman who had 22 kids? She tried to get her husband a job in a saw mill!

One cat jumped up onto a wall, beside her friend, and said, 'What would you like for Christmas?'

The other cat said, 'I'd like six lovely little kittens. What about you?'

The first one said, 'Yes, me too. I'd like a litter of about seven or eight.'

Just then a big Ginger Tom strolled round the corner, overheard them both, and said, 'Don't look now, girls, but here comes Santa Claus.'

A fellow went into a bar, and shouted 'Give me a gin.'

The barman gave him the gin. He then took an Oxo cube out of his pocket and put it in the drink.

The barman said, 'What do you call that?'

He said: 'Oxogin.'

My wife is a terrible cook. I bought a lovely bird for Christmas. A big fat turkey. I plucked it and stuffed it. And all the wife had to do was kill it and put it in the oven . . . and she couldn't even do that!

I was sitting in front of the telly on Christmas Eve, watching *Magic Roundabout*, when there was a tap on my shoulder. It was the Christmas turkey. It stood there, shivering, and said, 'Look mate, either light that gas-oven, or give me my feathers back . . . I'm freezing to death.'

A club I went to play last week, up North. It was like Aberdeen on a flag day . . .
I went up to the bar. I said, 'How's business?'
The manager said, 'Bad.'
I ordered a double whisky, and said, 'How much is that?'
The manager said, 'Have it on me, son, and let the New Year in.'

We invited the mother-in-law over for Christmas dinner. Eat? You've never seen anything like it. She's got starting-blocks on her elbows . . . I've never seen racing colours on a knife and fork before!

Eleven years I've been married. And it seems like only yesterday. I wish it was tomorrow – I'd cancel it!

I remember my wedding day. My mate Fred said, 'Alan, will it be a white wedding?'
I said, 'Yes – if it snows.'

My wife was an ice-cream girl in the cinema before I married her. On our wedding day, she walked down the aisle backwards. . . .

We got to the altar steps. She was all in white. I was white and all in.

We spent our honeymoon in Blackpool. A place called the Bare Hotel. The tables were bare, the walls were bare, and the chambermaids were . . . lovely!

I went to the pictures the other day to see a Western. I sat so near the screen, they made me Sheriff three times.

They had an electric power cut in America once. A fellow was sentenced to death and was in the electric chair, when suddenly all the power was cut off. . . . They had to finish him off with a blow lamp!

My little lad came in last week and said, 'Can I ask you a question, Dad – where did I come from?'

So I spent an hour-and-a-half giving him a lecture on the birds and the bees, and getting into a right old mix-up I was.

Finally, he said, 'Thanks, Dad.'

He was on his way out, and I asked, 'Anyway, what made you ask that question?'

He said, 'I just wanted to know – 'cos little Horace from next door said he comes from Blackpool.'

My lad won't get his hair cut. He hates going to the barber's, but I did manage to get him there last week. The barber was cutting away, and he said suddenly, 'Tell me son, do you go to the grammar school?'

He said, 'Yes, how do you know?'

The Barber said, 'I've just found your cap.'

I go to Manchester regularly to see my mother-in-law . . . She lives in Liverpool, actually. But she looks better from Manchester!

A Scotman got on a bus in London, put his suitcase under the stairs and said, 'The Houses of Parliament, please!'

The conductor said, 'Five pence, and two pence for the suitcase.'

The Scot said, 'I'm not paying that for a suitcase.'

The conductor said, 'If you don't pay up, I'm going to throw the suitcase off the bus.'

The Scotsman still refused to pay. So the conductor picked up the case, and threw it off the bus – straight into the River Thames.

The Scot was livid. He yelled and screamed: 'You're not satisfied with trying to rob me, you English swindler, but you're also trying to drown my wee boy as well.'

Photo: John Herring

Chapter Eighteen
TONY STEWART

TONY STEWART, 'born and bred in the Gorbals', keeps the flag flying for Scotland on the TV show.

His first job as an entertainer was with Pinder's No. 1 Royal Circus, touring Scotland as a clown. 'I used to fetch the water and clean the horses whenever the circus came near my home town,' he says. 'Then, one summer, Harry Savone, who was the principal clown, asked me if I would like to join them for the season.

'I told him I'd have to ask my mother. Luckily, she agreed. So I went to work for them for £3 a week and my keep.'

Tony's life with the circus took him all over Scotland. ('I shared a caravan with a baboon. I was in the cage most of the time, and he was free,' he jokes . . . 'He was a very nice animal. He used to throw bananas at me – but only when I'd forgotten to take him for a walk. We were great friends, really.')

In the circus, Tony learned to ride a horse in the ring, and he also did an acrobatic act, hanging from two rings. Then he had a spell working as a clown . . . white face, red nose, baggy trousers. Behind the heavy make-up, no one realised he had not long left school.

After the circus, Tony joined the Merchant Navy. He spent a year at sea. But there was only one slight problem . . . **he**

141

suffered from sea-sickness! But it was while he was at sea, that he built up a comedy act, entertaining the crew with jokes and impressions.

Back on land, he worked as a lifeguard on the beach at Roker, Sunderland, a 'bouncer' at the Lyceum Ballroom in the Strand, London, and then a travelling salesman, trying to sell vacuum cleaners. ('I used to always try and get the customers laughing. Then, before they stopped, I'd sold them a vacuum cleaner').

Tony's grandfather was a professional music-hall entertainer, and he reckons some of the talent rubbed off onto him. Grand-dad Kearney (Tony's real surname) was in the original Fred Karno company, touring the music halls. Then Karno had an offer to go to America to make some silent films, as the movie industry was just starting up in sunny California.

But Mrs. Kearney senior told him: 'If you go to America, you won't have a wife and family when you come back.' So he decided to stay in this country, and his place was eventually taken in the troupe by another music-hall comic – by the name of Stan Laurel. He went on, of course, to team up with Oliver Hardy and become one of the greatest comedy double acts of all time.

'My grandfather used to tell me fascinating stories of people like Hetty King, Gertie Gitana and Florrie Forde, and other great music hall performers of the Victorian era,' says Tony, whose father, Stewart Kearney, was also a performer, but in a very different sphere. He laid claim to being the world's champion pipe-band drummer.

It was Ronnie Culbertson, one of the five Smith Brothers, a singing group who used to perform in full Scottish dress, who first encouraged Tony to become a professional entertainer. He recommended him to Issy Bonn, the agent, who promptly signed him up in 1962 and put Tony into his first summer season – at Newquay – with ventriloquist Ray Alan topping the bill.

'I received ten quid a week,' says Tony, 'plus an extra four pounds for cleaning out the theatre, washing the floors, and emptying the ash trays. But it was all tremendous experience.'

His first TV came with Yorkshire's *Jokers Wild*. Since then, he's toured South Africa three times, been to Australia, and had a summer season in Jersey.

In cabaret, Tony is more of an all-round entertainer than just a stand-up comic. 'I do impressions and throw-away bits. . . . a cod striptease and an impression of a ventriloquist with two dolls.'

Invariably he finishes his act with 'Donald, Where's Your Troosers?', the Scottish song made famous by Andy Stewart, his namesake.

Naturally, his humour is sprinkled liberally with gags about the Scots, and their notorious meanness. 'There is a wealth of material about how mean the Scots are,' he says, 'and we do have a sense of humour North o' the Border, and the ability to laugh at ourselves.'

───────

We're not really as mean in Scotland as a lot of people think . . . But, as a Scot, I must say I like coming to England . . . when you get stuck in a traffic jam, you get pushed, so you save on petrol!

Normally, I'm right-handed . . . so I keep my money in my left-hand pocket.

I took my money out of the bank for a holiday – after it had one, I put it back again!

I was squeezing a tube of toothpaste the other day, and I accidentally twisted my ankle!

Three Scotsmen sitting together in Church. The parson said, 'I want everyone to put £1 on the collection plate this morning.' One of the Scots fainted, and the other two quickly carried him out.

I came down to Manchester. I'm staying in a very nice hotel. The towels are lovely and fluffy and big . . . So fluffy and big I could hardly shut my suitcase!

A Scotsman took his family into a restaurant, and they all had sausages, egg and chips. After the meal there were two sausages left on a plate.
The Scot said, 'I'll take them home for the dog.'
And one of the kids shouted, 'Whoooopeee! . . . we're going to get a dog!'

There was a daring smash-and-grab raid in Aberdeen last week.

The robbers would have got away with it, but they went back for the brick.

I went into the Barber's shop. I said, 'How much is a haircut?'
He said, 'Twenty-five new pence.'
I said, 'How much is a shave?'
He said, 'Fifteen new pence.'
I said, 'Right, then shave my head.'

This Scots fellow was up in court before the Judge.
Judge: 'You are accused of stealing a car. How do you plead?'
He said, 'Not guilty.'
Judge: 'Why not? You took the car, didn't you?'
He said, 'Well, I saw the car parked outside the cemetery, and I thought the owner was dead.'

I love coming to places like Manchester. Especially visiting restaurants . . . because whenever I sit down at a table, I keep finding money under the plates!

A woman went to the cemetery. She said to the head gardener, 'I'd like to see my husband's grave.'
He said, 'What's his name?'
She said, 'Brown.'
He said, 'What's his first name?'
She said, 'Angus.'
He said, 'We've got no Angus Brown in here, madam. The only Brown I can think of buried here is a Maggie Brown.'
She said, 'Oh, that's him, everything's in my name.'

I knew a Scotsman once, he was so mean. Well, one day he came out of his house and he saw this poor tramp eating the grass on his front lawn. He said, 'What are you doing there?'
The tramp said, 'I'm starving. I'm so hungry, I'm eating your grass.'
The Scotsman said, 'Oh come on now, round to the back garden – the grass is much longer there.'

Hear about the hippy who took prune juice with his LSD?
What a trip he took!

I went into a golf club and asked for a caddie. A young fellow came round. I said, 'Are you a caddie?'

He said, 'I am.'
I said, 'Are you any good at finding balls?'
He said, 'Yes, I am. Very good.'
I said, 'Good. Well, go and find me one, and maybe I can go out and have a game.'

Two pigeons flying over a racecourse. One says to the other: 'Who do you fancy for the big race?'
The other pigeon says, 'Oh, I'm going to put everything I've got on Lester Piggott.'

This fellow's wife died. They are going through the cemetery gates with the coffin, when one of the bearers accidentally bumps the coffin on the gate-post. There was a knocking noise from inside the coffin. So they took it back to the house, opened it up and they found the woman wasn't dead at all. She had been in a deep coma. So she got up – and lived for another nine years. Then she died.
So they're going through the cemetery gates with the coffin again, and as they walk in, the husband goes through first and says to the bearers: 'Fellers, watch out for that wee gate post – don't bump it again!'

Three men in a maternity hospital, waiting for news. The nurse comes out, goes to one fellow and says, 'Is this your baby?'
He takes a look at it, and shakes his head.
She says to the next man, 'Is this your baby?' He looks at it, and says, 'No, that's not mine.'
The third fellow goes over, looks down at the baby, which is black, and says: 'It must be mine. That wife of mine burns everything!'

A Scotsman is lying in bed, thinking 'What can I buy my wife for her birthday?'
He turns to her and says, 'Maggie, what do you want for your birthday tomorrow?'
She says, 'Lor, why are you lying awake worrying about a thing like that for? I'd like a surprise, anyway.'
So they both went to sleep. And at five o'clock next morning, he yelled at her, 'Boo!'

A Scotsman was on holiday in America, and he looks up at a statue of George Washington, but doesn't know who it is.

He stops an American, and says, 'Hey, excuse me, can you tell me who that is?'

The Yank says, 'That, sir, is George Washington, first President of the USA. When he was president of the United States, not a lie passed his lips.'

The Scotsman said, 'Is that a fact? Then he must have talked through his nose, like the rest of you!'

I'd better go now, because I'm double parked at a meter . . . My car's on top of George Roper's!

A cannibal sets up a restaurant in the middle of the African jungle, and puts up a menu with his charges:

Boiled Englishman	—	*20 pence.*
Boiled Irishman	—	*20 pence.*
Boiled Welshman	—	*20 pence.*
Boiled Hippy	—	*£3-50 pence.*

A customer came in, read the menu and said, 'Why do you charge so much for a hippy?'

The cannibal chef said, 'Have you ever tried to clean one?'

Chapter Nineteen
DUGGIE BROWN

THIS FELLOW *has a parrot and he's teaching it to speak, but all the parrot will say is: 'Who is it?'*
Well, the chap goes to work one morning, and at 9.30 a.m., there is a knock on the front door. The parrot screeches: 'Who is it?'
The man at the door says: 'It's the plumber. I've come to mend your pipes, will you let me in please?'
And the parrot says: 'Who is it?'
He says, 'It's the plumber. I've come to mend your pipes, will you let me in please?'
The parrot says: 'Who is it?'
And he says, 'It's the plumber. I've come to mend your pipes, will you let me in please?'
And the parrot says: 'Who is it?'
The fellow gets a bit upset, and he shouts: 'It's the plumber. I've come to mend your pipes, will you let me in please?'

Duggie Brown reckons he is not a very funny fellow, away from *The Comedians*. But he enjoys 'playing the spoons' – with only one spoon!
He's now put this little bit of nonsense into his stage act. He

147

simply walks on with one spoon and starts 'playing' it. ('You'd be surprised what kind of tunes you can get out of playing the spoon,' he says, still trying to be serious. 'It's just like playing an out-of-tune piano . . . only it sounds better!')

Nevertheless, when he was playing the spoon on stage at a club in Wales, one lady from the audience came to him afterwards and said, 'Wouldn't you be better off with two spoons? Y'know, we couldn't hear a thing from where we were sitting!')

There is a knack to it, which Duggie is very reluctant to divulge. For he has a very musical background.

He was born in Rotherham, Yorkshire, and started, even before he left school, playing with a skiffle group. At 15, he formed a group with three other blokes. They won a competition at the Continental Palace, Hull, and consequently found their way onto the *6.5 Special* BBC TV show.

Duggie played guitar. The others were Bill Brown, Barrie Winder and George Payling, and they stayed together as a music group for twelve years, which must have been something of a record in the pop business.

They started out as *The Four Imps*, changed their name to *The Four Kool-Katz*, and then to *The Douglas Brown Four* – just to sound posh. They earned quite a name for themselves, particularly in Scotland, where they were based for some years.

'We were a very visual group, with a lot of action,' says Duggie. 'In between the music, we did lots of impersonations – Andy Stewart, the Alexander Brothers, Fyfe Robertson, Robin Hall and Jimmy McGregor.' If it was Scottish and it moved, the Douglas Brown Four quickly impersonated it!

He moved back to Yorkshire after getting married (his wife Margaret was a dancer in Scotland) and he wanted to bring up their young daughter, Jacqueline, in his native Yorkshire.

Because he wanted to try his luck as a solo artist, the group split up, and Duggie went off to the Yorkshire working-men's clubs, under the name of Douglas Browne (although his real name is Barry Douglas Dudley). He was then a singer, who played the guitar and just told a few jokes in between his songs.

His sister, Lynne Perrie, who is an actress as well as a cabaret artist (she's appeared in *Coronation Street* and Yorkshire TV's *Queenie's Castle*) recommended Duggie to an agent, and he quickly advised the lad to concentrate more on the comedy side of his act.

The big breakthrough came when, one night, he forgot the tag line for one of his jokes, and spluttered, on stage, trying to think of how to finish the gag. The audience laughed so much that he hit on the idea of deliberately forgetting his jokes in future.

It has since worked a treat, and he now deliberately gives the impression of forgetting most of his jokes halfway through.

So the parrot screeched: 'Who is it?'
And the man at the door shouted: 'It's the plumber. I've come to mend your pipes, will you let me in please?'
And the parrot said: 'Who is it?'
And the man said, 'It's the plumber. I've come to mend your pipes, will you let me in please?' . . . very angrily.

He also has a habit of spreading out his jokes in a long-winded fashion. 'They're not so much jokes, as long, drawn-out anecdotes and funny stories.'

Really, he has a good memory for gags. 'My first real experience as a professional comedian came when I was asked to do a 25-minute spot, telling gags at a club. To me, at that time, 25 minutes seemed like a summer season!'

But, somehow, he got through it – at the Windmill Club, Leeds. And he's had audiences in Yorkshire and surrounding areas howling with mirth ever since.

His deliberate forgetfulness can sometimes rebound, however. A couple of years ago, one club manager who had booked him for £20 for the night went to see Duggie's agent, and said: 'I saw this lad Duggie Brown in another club, and he forgot half his jokes. He's useless. I want to cancel my booking of him.'

'I like "taking the mickey",' says Duggie mischievously. He has a friendly, relaxed style, and the secret, he reckons, is that when he gets up on stage he is just like 'one of the blokes from the audience, getting up to do a turn.'

He has no nerves, he says. 'I just go tired, instead. So I don't tremble . . . I just sleep it off and have a quiet snooze'.

His only TV appearance, prior to *The Comedians* last year, was in the BBC's *Good Old Days*. ('I told a few gags, sang a few snatches of "Marta", and wore a hired suit of green tweed. But I split my pants right down the middle, just before I went on stage – and I had only three safety pins keeping me from appearing in court').

Duggie was the winner, in 1969, of *The Stage* annual award as Best Comedy act in the clubs. It was on this occasion that Johnnie Hamp first saw him.

Apart from telling gags, he still plays the guitar and the piano in his stage act (and plays both out of tune, just to keep the audiences guessing!). 'It's funny,' he says. 'They never quite know whether I'm simply not very good, or whether it's deliberate.' That's his story, anyway.

'Like most other comics, I've died at some clubs,' he admits. 'I was once slow-handclapped at Middlesbrough. I had to follow The Tremeloes, and I went on and played the spoons (only one, remember!). I can honestly say I was not a great success that night. In fact, I was tremendously relieved to get away from the place with all my limbs still intact.'

Despite his enormous success on the TV show, he still has reservations about playing certain towns which are notorious for not liking comics. 'After all, I can find clubs nearer home that don't like me, without travelling hundreds of miles to find 'em.'

Two coloured chaps in Birmingham, Alabama, and one says:
'Rastus, what would you do if you got a letter from the Ku Klux Klan, telling you to leave town?'
Rastus says: 'I'd read it on the train'.

But Duggie has an extra string to his bow. He is now an accomplished actor, as well as a clown. His first acting part was in the film *Kes*, where he had a small role as a milkman.

There he met actor-writer Colin Welland, and consequently appeared in Colin's TV plays *Slattery's Mounted Foot* and *Say Goodnight To Your Grandma*, and in Jack Rosenthal's Granada play *Another Sunday – And Sweet F.A*.

He is also in the new feature film *For The Love Of Ada*, playing a barber, called Duggie Brown. ('Just in case I should forget who I was').

He sees no reason at all why he should not mix straight acting parts with his role as a comedian, and now wants to establish himself as a TV situation comedian – another opportunity which looks like coming his way, thanks to his performances in *The Comedians*.

His only interest outside of show business, he says, is drinking (and he does that, like most drinkers, simply to avoid dying of thirst!) and golf. He plays off a handicap of 18.

He did a round in 69, and another in 71. . . . He's hoping to have another game in 1974!

. . . And the parrot screeches: 'Who is it?'

The man at the door yells back: 'It's the plumber. I've come to mend your pipes, will you let me in please?'

This goes on for five hours, with the plumber and the parrot screaming at each other. In the end, the blood pressure gets the better of him, and the plumber collapses in a heap on the doorstep. Well, at five o'clock in the evening, the man comes home from work, and he trips over this body.

And he yells: 'Who is it?'

And the parrot screeches back: 'It's the plumber. He's come to mend your pipes, will you let him in please?'

This woman was learning French, and the coalman called. She thought she'd practise a bit of French on him. So she said: 'Four hundredweight, s'il vous plait.'

The coalman was quick. He said, 'Certainly madam. How would you like it? A la-carte? Or cul-de-sac?'

A ventriloquist wasn't doing so well, so he bought himself a crystal ball, a turban and a cloak, and set up as a medium.

This woman came in and said, 'My husband died three years ago, and I'd like to make contact with him. Can you help?'

He said, 'Oh aye, I can.'

She said, 'Well how much will it cost me?'

He said, 'Well, it will cost you five guineas if you hear his voice, ten guineas if you want to hold a lengthy conversation with him. Or fifty guineas if you want to talk to him while I'm drinking a glass of water.'

I think Georgie Best has changed, hasn't he? He's gone big-headed. He won't play for Manchester United, he won't play for Ireland. . . . He only wants to play with Miss United Kingdom!

I'm glad India and Pakistan have signed a Peace Treaty. Now the road from Leeds to Bradford can open again.

A drunk came home late one night, staggered up the stairs, into the bedroom, took off all his clothes and paraded in front of the open window. His wife woke up, saw him and shouted: 'For goodness sake, Fred, will you get into bed, before the neighbours see you? . . . They'll think I only married you for your money!'

I support Doncaster Rovers. But they sold half their team, the best four or five, to the Italian club Juventus. And Fray Bentos want the rest of 'em!

This drunk was staggering around a fairground. He came to the rifle range, pulled out ten pence and decided to have a go. They gave him a gun, and he shot down all the targets. The lady said 'Very good', and she gave him a prize – a baby tortoise.
He went away. Half an hour later he was back again. 'Here, I'll have another go.'
He paid his tenpence, got the rifle, shot all the targets down again.
'You've won again,' said the lady, 'Here's a prize', and she gave him a little chalk doll.
The drunk said, 'I don't want that. I want the same as I won last time . . . a meat pie with a hard crust.'

Two Irish football teams playing a match. The referee, another Irish bloke, calls the two captains together before the start, looks up at the sky and says, 'Look lads, I think it's going to get foggy later, so we'll play the extra time first, okay?'

A fellow was about to be executed in France in the olden days . . .
He was just standing by the guillotine, when a messenger came dashing up and said, 'Excuse me, here's a letter for you.'
He said, 'Put it in the basket . . . I'll read it later.'

Income Tax is made very simple these days, isn't it?
They only ask you three questions:
    A. How much did you earn last year?
    B. How much have you got left?
    C. Will you please send it?

An Irish navvy was digging a hole in the road. The foreman said, 'Where are you going to put all the dirt from that hole?' So the navvy started digging another hole. He said, 'I'll put it in here.'
The foreman said, 'But surely you'll have some dirt from the second hole, won't you?'
He said, 'Oh no, 'cos I'm digging this hole deeper.'

An American was driving his Cadillac through a tiny Irish village. He stopped at a railway level-crossing, and looked up at the signal-box. One gate was open, and the other gate was closed. The signalman explained: 'When we are expecting a train, sir, we close the gates, so that there won't be a crash.'

The American said, 'Yes, I can appreciate that. But why have you got one gate open, and one closed?'

The Irishman said, 'Ah well, sir, we're only half expecting a train today.'

A fellow went to see the psychiatrist.

He said, 'I've come about my brother. He thinks he's an orange.'

Psychiatrist: 'Well, where is he?'

He said: 'He's in my pocket.'

I've got a brother at Manchester University. He's in the laboratories there. Well, actually, he's in a bottle – because he's got two heads!

I've another brother with three heads. He's in the police force. He goes around saying, 'Hello! hello! hello!'

I used to have a good job in Bradford . . . I rode shotgun on a Kit-e-Kat delivery wagon!

I've been on the dole so long, they even sent me a ticket for their staff dance . . . And now they're going to show my working boots on *All Our Yesterdays*.

Chapter Twenty

A LAST LAUGH

JACKIE HAMILTON

A fellow went into a toy-shop . . .
'How much is that little boat in the window?'
Assistant: 'Five pounds- 50 pence!'
He said: 'That's a bit expensive, isn't it? I thought there was a
sale on?'
Assistant: 'No, it goes by a little battery inside.'

A pal of mine was standing at the bus-stop, eating fish and chips,
and looking absolutely fed-up. I said, 'What's the matter with
you, Charlie?'
He said: 'I'll tell you what's the matter with me, mate. I lost all
my wages this afternoon on the horses, I came home and found
the wife had left home, gone off with the milkman. She's broken
into the gas meter and taken every penny in the house, and left
me with the six kids. I'm so fed up, I've decided that the next
bus that comes along, I'm going to throw myself under it.'
I said, 'Surely things can't be that bad. Anyway, what's the idea
of eating fish and chips in the street?'
He said, 'Blimey, you'd starve around here, waiting for a ruddy
bus.'

A little boy goes to his mother and says: 'Mum, how do buffaloes make love?'
His mother said: 'I don't know, son. Your father's a Mason.'

BAL MOANE

A little Irish fellow went to the Doctor's.
The Doctor said, 'Murphy, have you 'flu?'
He said, 'No, I've come on my bike.'

JOHNNY (GOON) TWEED

A supermarket was broken into in Manchester yesterday, and 5,000 cigarettes and twelve dozen lettuces were stolen. The police are now looking for a rabbit with a bad cough.

Two prisoners escaped from Walton Jail, Liverpool, yesterday. One was seven feet six inches tall, and the other fellow was only four feet nine.
The police are looking high and low for them.

MIKE COYNE

Hear about the Mermaid who was pregnant? It was an act of Cod!

EDDIE FLANAGAN

A Chinaman saw an advert on the telly- 'Go to work on an egg!'
So he went and bought an egg, and he joined the AA.
Next day, he was all set to go to work on his egg, but it wouldn't move. So he phoned up the AA headquarters and told them he couldn't get to work because his egg wouldn't start, could they come and see it right away?
The AA man thought 'Hello, someone is having a joke with me here.'
So he said to the Chinaman, 'Try pulling your yoke out.'
The Chinaman rang back ten minutes later, 'I've pulled the yoke out – and it's all white now!'